THE CROSS OF CHRIST

The
Cross of Christ

A.B. Simpson

CHRISTIAN PUBLICATIONS
CAMP HILL, PENNSYLVANIA

Christian Publications
3825 Hartzdale Drive, Camp Hill, PA 17011

The mark of ✝ *vibrant faith*

ISBN: 0-87509-527-5
LOC Catalog Card Number: 93-74749
© 1994 by Christian Publications
All rights reserved
Printed in the United States of America

94 95 96 97 98   5   4   3   2   1

CONTENTS

The Kaleidoscope of the Cross

The people stood watching. (Luke 23:35)

What varied thoughts and feelings moved the hearts of those who stood that day beholding the cross of Calvary! We can perceive the cruel heartlessness with which the Roman soldiers drove the nails and reared the cross, interested only in getting their share of the petty spoil for which they cast lots. We can conceive of the fiendish ferocity with which the rulers and chief priests gloated over the agony of their victim and felt themselves at last avenged. We can comprehend the heartbreak with which those loving women looked upon the helpless anguish of the One in whom they had so much believed. We can realize something of that mother's grief as she recalled the words of Simeon thirty years before: "and a sword will pierce your own soul too" (Luke 2:35). We can imagine that Peter, gazing from afar upon the tragedy, would have given worlds to have taken back that last dart with which he had pierced his Master's heart, but realized that now he would see Him no more. And we know something from the narrative of the awe and veneration with which the Roman centurion gazed upon the extraordinary signs which accompanied His death and exclaimed, "Surely this man was the Son of God!" (Mark 15:39).

And so they stood beholding. And all through the ages generations after generations have turned their eyes to that central cross as it has loomed larger and loftier above all other spectacles in the vision of the human race. Once more Christ is set forth before us, crucified among us, and faith and love once more stand beholding. As we gaze upon that scene so old and yet so ever new, it seems as if that cross appears like some vision in a kaleidoscope. With every turn the holy Scriptures show some new light and some different aspect of its many-sided glory and significance. Let us follow the holy Scriptures as they present to us some of these varied phases of the cross of Jesus.

A Death Scene

Death is always an impressive spectacle, but this was no ordinary death. Here was a Man who did not need to die, but One who chose to die, One who came to die, One whose supreme mission was to die, One over whose cross each of us can write, "He died for me."

A Crucifixion

This is more than an ordinary death scene, for He "became obedient to death—even death on a cross" (Philippians 2:8). Crucifixion was adopted by the Romans as the severest form of capital punishment. It was the most agonizing and it was the most shameful of all deaths. What agony was endured as every muscle was strained to its utmost tension, as the helpless body hung by its own weight from lacerated flesh and bones, slowly dying from sheer anguish with no vital organ wounded, as the crucible of pain burned up by slow degrees life's last powers of endurance! How pitiful was the cry of the crucified Savior as it was foreshadowed in the prophetic Psalm:

> I am poured out like water,
>   and all my bones are out of joint.
> My heart has turned to wax;
>   it has melted away within me.
> My strength is dried up like a potsherd,
>   and my tongue sticks to the roof of
>   my mouth;
> you lay me in the dust of death.
>   (Psalm 22:14–15)

And what shame was suffered as He hung there, crucified between two thieves. He was treated not only as one of them, but worse than either. His very name was blotted out of the family records at Bethlehem, and He was looked upon by men and even treated by His own Father as if He were the worst and vilest criminal that ever lived or died.

A Murder

"You, with the help of wicked men, put him to death by nailing him to the cross" (Acts 2:23). "You handed him over to be killed, and you disowned him before Pilate, though he had decided to let him go" (3:13). It was a judicial assassination. He was God's martyred Lamb, and our martyred Master.

A Voluntary Sacrifice

Jesus said of His own death, "The good shepherd lays down his life for the sheep" (John 10:11). "I lay down my life for the sheep. . . . I have authority to lay it down and authority to take it up again" (10:15, 18). He gave Himself for us. "No one takes it from me, but I lay it down of my own accord" (10:18). As He hung upon that cross, even death could not come till He said, "It is finished" (19:30), and bowed His head, as if beckoning death to come, and "gave up his spirit" (19:30). Was there ever a death like this? Human nature flees from death as the worst of all evils. But here was a Man who from the beginning to the end of His life had one supreme object—to lay down His own life for the sake of others.

A Baptism

"I have a baptism to undergo, and how distressed I am until it is completed!" (Luke 12:50). It was ever present to His thoughts. It was ever calling Him to the cross. It was ever coloring every act and object of His life. It was ever casting its shadow over His consciousness so that He died a thousand deaths before He even approached the cross.

A Passion

"After his suffering, he showed himself to these men" (Acts 1:3). Literally, the word passion means suffering. But it conveys the idea of intense suffering, suffering that involved His inner as well as His outer being, His soul and spirit as well as His rent body. It is true that His "soul [was] overwhelmed with sorrow to the point of death" (Matthew 26:38).

A Travail

Travail is considered the severest form of human agony, and thus represents in the most emphatic light the excruciating anguish of the Savior's death. But it speaks of more than agony. It has in it the silver lining of hope and life and promise. It is the birth pang of a new creation. "When her baby is born she forgets the anguish because of her joy that a child is born into the world" (John 16:21). And so there was a joy even in the Savior's agony, and already the promise came to Him. "He will see his offspring and will prolong his days, and the will of the LORD will prosper in his hand. After the suffering of his soul, he will see the light of life and be satisfied" (Isaiah 53:10–11).

A Decree

"They spoke about his departure [decease, KJV], which he was about to bring to fulfillment at Jerusalem" (Luke 9:31). Decease is more than death. It means an outgoing, a departure, and carries with it the idea of a future life and a continued activity. So He changed the sphere of His existence and passed through the gates of death in a higher and more glorious ministry.

A Planting

"If we have been united with him like this in his death, we will certainly also be united with him in his resurrection" (Romans 6:5). This figure has an added charm in the beautiful conjunction of the Easter season and the Spring when all nature is alive with illustrations and types of the new creation. The figure of planting is very different from that of burying. It is not a grave plot, but a garden. You do not drop the lifeless remains of some loved one into the gloomy grave; you simply put away a living seed with the confidence that it will come forth in beauty in shoot and bud and blossom and fruit. And so the death of Christ was just a glorious planting, and every time we die with Him, we are just making a great investment, from which we are going to reap some day a hundredfold. Let me not be afraid to let the "kernel of wheat [fall] to the ground and [die]," for "if it dies, it produces many seeds" (John 12:24).

A Lifting Up

"Just as Moses lifted up the snake in the desert, so the Son of Man must be lifted up" (3:14). "When you have lifted up the Son of Man, then you will know that I am the one I claim to be" (8:28). "But I, when I am lifted up from the earth, will draw all men to myself" (12:32). The cross of Christ was intended for the eyes of the whole world. Let us lift Him up by our testimony, by our love, and in our adoring praise and worship until all the world shall stand beholding.

An Offering

The idea of an offering is something that pleases God. In Christ He beheld for the first time with perfect satisfaction the consecration of a human life. Even if no sinner had ever been saved it still would have been an offering well pleasing to God, "a fragrant offering and sacrifice" (Ephesians 5:2).

A Sacrifice

A sacrifice is different from an offering. It carries with it the idea of sin to be expiated, of substitution for the guilty, of atonement for the transgressions of men. So Christ died for sinners that they might not die, and suffered "the

righteous for the unrighteous, to bring you to
God" (1 Peter 3:18).

A Great Victory

On the cross He met Satan and overthrew him.
"Having disarmed the powers and authorities, he
made a public spectacle of them, triumphing over
them by the cross" (Colossians 2:15). And so we
are said to overcome by the blood of the Lamb.

An Example

> Christ suffered for you, leaving you an
> example, that you should follow in his
> steps. . . .
> When they hurled their insults at him,
> he did not retaliate; when he suffered,
> he made no threats. Instead, he
> entrusted himself to him who judges
> justly. He himself bore our sins in his
> body on the tree, so that we might die
> to sins and live for righteousness. (1
> Peter 2:21, 23–24)

The crucifixion was a great object lesson of
submission, gentleness, meekness and self surrender. "He was oppressed and afflicted, yet he
did not open his mouth; he was led like a lamb to
the slaughter" (Isaiah 53:7). Christ's death is
much more than this; but let us not forget this
also amid the suffering and trial through which
we follow Him.

A Ransom

Christ's death was the meeting of the conditions of that great covenant which the Father had made with His Son ages before, promising eternal life to all for whom He should pay this costly price. And now the price has been paid, the redemption accomplished, and the heirs of the covenant may come and claim as much as that blood is worth.

A Reconciliation

At Christ's cross God and the sinner can meet while Christ stands between, reaching out one pierced hand to the Father, pleading, "Father, forgive them, for they do not know what they are doing" (Luke 23:34), and the other to sinners beseeching, "Be reconciled to God" (2 Corinthians 5:20).

A Revelation

"God demonstrates his own love for us" not by talking about it, but by doing something which proves it, and commends it as no words could ever have done: "while we were still sinners, Christ died for us" (Romans 5:8).

A Pledge of the New Creation

Christ's cross is the pledge of the new creation for there old humanity died in the person of the seed of the woman, and new humanity was born in the person of the second Adam. And now, as we identify ourselves with Him, we are counted dead with Him to the curse of the law, to the dominion of the carnal nature, to the very center of our physical being and to the extent of the future resurrection itself. The reason I am justified is that the old sinner is dead with Christ, and I am no longer he, or liable for his sins. The reason I have victory over the power of sin is that in Christ I am dead to sin and I need no longer fear it or obey it. The reason I claim my healing in His name is that He has borne the liabilities of my body, and I can lay them over on Him who died for them. And by the same reason I am already anticipating the coming resurrection and triumphing over the fear and power of death. "If anyone is in Christ, he is a new creation; the old has gone, the new has come! All this is from God, who reconciled us to himself through Christ" (2 Corinthians 5:17–18).

An Inspiration

"For Christ's love compels us, because we are convinced that one died for all, and therefore all died. And he died for all, that those who live should no longer live for themselves but for him who died for them and was raised again" (5:14–15).

> I've got a word in my heart like a fire
>   That will not let me be;
> Jesus, the Son of God, who loved
>   And gave Himself for me.

If He'd loved and died for someone
    else,
  For Peter or blessed Paul;
If He'd loved and died for men like
    these,
  One wouldn't have wondered at all.

But 'twas for me that Jesus died,
  For me and a world of men,
Just as sinful, and just as slow,
  To give back His love again.

Did'st Thou love and die for a man
    like me?
  Then, Master, I will take
More thought for the perishing souls
    I meet,
  If it's only for Thy sake.

Identification

The cross of Christ demands from each of us identification. It is of no use to us unless we make it our own and enter into His death and resurrection. "In the same way, count yourselves dead to sin but alive to God in Christ Jesus" (Romans 6:11).

When Jesus died on Calvary,
  I, too, was there.
'Twas in my place He stood for me,
  And now accepted, even as He
His righteousness I share.

Under the Shadow
of the Cross

Do this in remembrance of me. (Luke 22:19)

This inscription placed by the hands of the Master over the Feast of Love might well be made the watchword of our whole Christian life. The Lord's Supper is a sort of microcosm, or miniature, of the believer's life. Over every moment, every word and every action we may well inscribe, "Do this in remembrance of me" (Luke 22:19).

After good Archbishop Darbly had been murdered by the Paris Communists, they found upon the walls of his dungeon the sketch of a rude cross, with these four words marking its extreme dimensions: *height, depth, length, breadth.* To his devout spirit the cross seemed to measure the love of God and the grace of Christ in its height and depth and length and breadth.

The arms of that cross are wide enough to cover every need and every experience of our daily lives. Its foundations are deeper than our deepest sorrows, and our loftiest heights of rapture can never reach above its heavenly altitude. It is God's measure not only of His love, but of our lives.

The medieval saints used to erect, in the center of the market square of every town, a simple cross, so that it came to be known as the Market Cross; and it may still be seen in many of the older towns of Europe. The simple and beautiful idea was that the cross should dominate all the business of earthly life, and that all transactions, interests and concerns should be under the shadow of the cross.

"Under the shadow of the cross"—how much this phrase suggests of sweetness, sacredness and practical consecration. Perhaps you are wearing a cross around your neck. Does the heart that throbs beneath it beat true to its holy meaning? Are the words that come from that throat, whose necklace is clasped by the symbol of His gentleness and suffering, in keeping with the cross you have to wear? Are the habiliments of your person and the habits of your life suggestive of Him whose only marks of honor were the thorn cuts, the spear gash and the blood of agony on Calvary?

Let us contemplate the cross in its practical relation to our actual Christian life.

Refuge for the Sinner

When the sinner comes to the deep and awful sense of his guilt and peril, what refuge can he find apart from the cross of Calvary? "Thus far did I come, laden with my sin," wrote Bunyan, telling the story of the sinner's refuge. Then as the strings broke and the burdens rolled away, there came the joyful song of praise,

> Blest Cross! Blest Sepulchre! Blest
>   rather be
> The Man that there was put to shame
>   for me.

Refuge for the Tempted

When temptation comes and the newborn soul has found its first stumbling stone, what can bring deliverance and victory but the cross of Calvary? And oh, what new light comes as the soul begins to fully realize that Christ has purchased for it not merely a brief reprieve or a new probation, but a complete and everlasting vindication. Our sins have not only been forgiven, but obliterated; in fact, they have ceased to be our sins and have been assumed by the great Sin Bearer. We are henceforth as free from liability for them as if we had never sinned! In the death of Calvary we have died, and we stand before the judgment and the high court of heaven in the position of those who have paid the full penalty for sin already and who, looking up in the face of heaven, can say, "Who will bring any charge against those whom God has chosen? It is God who justifies. Who is he that condemns? Christ Jesus, who died—more than that, who was raised to life—is at the right hand of God" (Romans 8:33–34).

Salvation from the Effects of Sin

Sometimes our past comes back again like great ocean billows threatening to overwhelm us. It is then that the cross rises as a mighty barrier and breakwater, even as rocks resist the billows around their shores, and we find that instead of reaping the harvest of our evil sowing, there is One who has reaped the wretched issue for us and we are free. We do not have to pass through the processes of natural law or pay the full penalty which sin exacts in the present life; but we may claim complete deliverance from the wreck of body and brain, and from temporal conditions which might justly have been our heritage, and go forth into a life as glorious and free as if we had just dropped from heaven, the new creation of infinite love.

Sanctification through the Cross

When we come to the great conflict with inbred sin we find once more that the cross has made provision not only for our justification but also for our sanctification. We do not have to fight alone the demon of depravity in our own hearts or slowly build up out of the wreckage of the past a holy character. But we find that the old man, as well as the old deeds, was crucified with Him, and that it is our privilege to lay off the nature of self and sin and put on the very nature and life of Christ Himself "who has become for us wisdom from God—that is, our righteousness, holiness and redemption" (1 Corinthians 1:30). And as the process of grace goes deeper and reveals to us yet undiscovered depths of corruption, we shall find that the cross is deeper still. With every new revelation we may continue to put off the "old self with its practices and have put on the new self" (Colossians 3:9–10) in a loftier resurrection life, as step by step we come to "know Christ and the power of his resurrection and the fellowship of sharing in his sufferings, becoming like him in his death" (Philippians 3:10).

Healing through the Cross

Still further we slowly learn that the shadow of that cross touches our mortal frame, that our very bodies have been redeemed, that our liability to sickness because of sin has been canceled by His death, that we may lay over our sicknesses and infirmities upon Him who bore them, and that we may take His resurrection life for every physical need of this mortal frame. "He was pierced for our transgressions, he was crushed for our iniquities; the punishment that brought us peace was upon him, and by his wounds we are healed" (Isaiah 53:5).

Fellowship with His Cross

Much of our life contains suffering and trial, and the shadow of the cross is also here. Looking upon our trials as unmeaning accidents, the blow of fate, the luck of evil fortune or the cruel wrongs of men and women is so different from taking them from our Father's hand as the cup of His loving discipline and as the fellowship of our Savior's cross! How we have striven sometimes with some tremendous sorrow, and have refused to bow our head as it grew darker and more dreadful and as the iron of despair entered our nerveless soul. Then at last a sweet message from the heart of God the Comforter has breathed the prayer of faith and submission, "Shall I not drink the cup the Father has given me?" (John 18:11). How the clouds melted away, and like a benediction there have fallen upon our hearts the precious words, "I have told you these things, so that in me you may have peace. In this world you will have trouble. But take heart! I have overcome the world" (16:33). And again the echo has fallen upon our ears, "Do not be surprised at the painful trial you are suffering, as though something strange were happening to you. But rejoice that you participate in the sufferings of Christ, so that you may be overjoyed when his glory is revealed" (1 Peter 4:12–13).

Ah, but you say, "People caused my sufferings." Well, did not people cause His? And that is the very thing which makes your fellowship with His cross complete. But again I hear you say, "Yes, but I am innocent of the things they say; I am misrepresented, lied about and persecuted." Was not that the very glory of His cross? Are you going to throw back on Him the burden which He has left for you to share? Yes, it is true that we may "fill up . . . what is still lacking in regard to Christ's afflictions, for the sake of his body, which is the church" (Colossians 1:24). You can never share the wrath of God for sin. That He bore alone. But He has left for you to carry with Him "the fellowship of sharing in his sufferings" (Philippians 3:10).

An old legend tells us that when He met Simon Peter fleeing from Rome to escape the fiery wrath of Nero, He asked him, "Whither goest thou?" Peter frankly answered and told of his flight, and then asked in turn, "Lord, whither goest Thou?" The answer came, "I am going to Rome to be crucified a second time, because My disciple Peter has run away from his cross." It is no wonder that Peter turned back from his flight and hastened with downward head to follow his dying Lord. Let us also return and follow the Crucified.

> Must Jesus bear the cross alone,
> And all the world go free?
> No there's a cross for everyone.
> And there's a cross for me.

But it will cease to be a cross when we are

sweetly conscious that He is bearing the other
end, and that we are suffering with Him now and
shall yet be glorified together.

Surely we may say, as we think of all these
things, "May I never boast except in the cross of
our Lord Jesus Christ, through which the world
has been crucified to me, and I to the world"
(Galatians 6:14).

> The cross, it takes our guilt away,
> It holds the fainting spirit up;
> It cheers with hope the gloomy day
> And sweetens every bitter cup.
> The balm of life, the cure of woe,
> The measure and the pledge of love,
> The sinner's refuge here below,
> The angels' theme in heaven above

Our Attitude to Others through the Cross

The cross is also practical and powerful in its
influence upon our ministry for others, our relation to the world and our work for God. How
differently we would think, speak and judge concerning our fellow Christians if we lived more
under the shadow of the cross.

A Christian lady once asked, "How can I be
delivered from the spirit of censorious judging
and severe speaking of the faults of others?" In
that moment came to me a revelation of the Lord
Jesus Christ bearing the sins of others and taking
them upon Himself. For us then to put our hands

upon them is really to crucify Him afresh and demand that He should suffer again for the things that He has already borne. The revelation was so unspeakably vivid that it came almost like a shock and whatever effect this truth may have had upon the heart and life of the friend in question, I will never forget the awful light in which it seemed to place the sin of uncharitableness, criticism and evil speaking. Is not this covered by such texts as this, "Who are you to judge someone else's servant?" (Romans 14:4). "Who will bring any charge against those whom God has chosen? . . . Who is he that condemns? Christ Jesus, who died" (8:33–34). Let us think and speak and love henceforth under the shadow of the cross.

Our Attitude to the World through the Cross

The apostle declares that through the cross he has been crucified unto the world and the world unto him. Is this true of us? Do we look upon this world as the enemy that murdered our Lord? Can we join hands with it in its Christless pleasures and godless ambitions any more than a sister could dance with the ruffian that had murdered her brother? The world crucified our Christ and to us henceforth it must be recognized as our foe. Indeed, by the death of Christ we have died to the world and are counted as men that have passed out of it and then come back to it in a second life as God's sent ones, commissioned to represent the Master here. We cannot do this if we stoop to the world's level. It is from our heavenly place of identity with Him that we may expect to lift it to the higher level.

The cross in the market place! Oh, what a difference it would make if the cross of Calvary dominated all our business dealings, all our social amusements, all our pleasures and all our plans! Avarice would not dare claim its graft. Pleasure would blush in its mad revel before that vision of Him who came not to seek enjoyment or gain, but rather to lay down His rights and give up His very life, not only as an example of righteousness, but as a sacrifice of love.

The Cross—the Inspiration of Zeal and Sacrifice

And oh, how poor our sacrifices and services for our Master and our fellowmen appear under the shadow of the cross! "He died for all, that those who live should no longer live for themselves but for him who died for them and was raised again" (2 Corinthians 5:15). The cross is the only inspiration of true benevolence, sacrifice and zeal for the salvation of men and the salvation of the world. If its mark has been placed upon us, then we are not our own; we are bought with a price. All we are and have belongs to Him, and the great sacrifice is little to give to Him.

A contemporary journal stated that during the last winter of the war in Manchuria the Japanese emperor, learning of the sufferings of his soldiers from the awful rigors of the Russian winter, was so distressed that he refused to allow the fires to be lighted in his palace, and he spent that winter in fellowship with the sufferings of his heroic army. Such was the spirit of Jesus when our race was in peril. Heaven could be to Him no longer heaven, but down from the seats of glory He hastened to share our sin and save our world. Oh, surely, we might watch with Him one hour, and count it joy to share the fellowship of His love by sacrifice and service for the salvation of men! Are we doing this? Has the cross put its mark upon our ministry, upon our gifts, upon our personal labors for Him and for the perishing around us and the unsaved in more distant lands? Well may we cry when we think of such love:

> Oh, for a passionate passion for souls!
> Oh, for the pity that yearns!
> Oh, for the love that loves unto death!
> Oh, for the fire that burns!

No Cross, No Crown

What significance will the cross have in connection with the crown? If anything is true, this is true: there will be nothing in heaven that does not have the mark of the cross upon it and has not passed through death and resurrection. Even the very earth and heavens must pass away, and a new heaven and a new earth emerge. There shall be no joy, there shall be no glory, there shall be no crown for us there that did not come from

some surrender, some sacrifice, some renunciation, some crucifixion here. God help us, therefore, to stamp upon all our life below and our
crown above the passion sign of the cross.

The Brand of the Cross

Finally, let no one cause me trouble, for I bear on my body the marks of Jesus. (Galatians 6:17)

The word "marks" in this text is translated by Rotherham, "brand marks." The word describes a mark that has been branded into the flesh, and suggests the idea of the cruel practice of certain nations in branding political offenders in the face with a badge of dishonor which never could be erased. The Greek word literally means "a stigma," and suggests a mark of reproach and shame. The apostle says that he bears in his body the branded scar which identifies him with Christ and His cross.

The kind of mark which he refers to is made plain by the verse almost immediately preceding. "May I never boast except in the cross of our

Lord Jesus Christ, through which the world has been crucified to me, and I to the world" (6:14). It is the cross of Christ which is the object at once of His shame and His glory. Let us look first at the marks of the Lord Jesus, and then at their reproduction in His followers.

The Cross Marks of Christ

He was always overshadowed by the cross which at last He bore on Calvary. His life was a life of humiliation and suffering from the manger to the tomb.

His birth was under a shadow of dishonor and shame. The shadow that fell upon the virgin mother could not be removed from her child, and even to this day only faith in a supernatural incarnation can explain away that reproach.

His childhood was overshadowed by sorrow. Soon after His birth, He was pressed by Herod with relentless hate. He spent His early childhood as an exile in the land of Egypt, which had always been associated in the history of His people as the house of bondage.

His early manhood was spent in toil and poverty and he was known all His later life as "the carpenter's son." A modern painter represents Him as under the shadow of the cross even in the early days at Nazareth; as He returns from a day of toil with arms outstretched with weariness, the setting sun flings the shadow of his figure across the pathway, suggestive of a dark cross.

His life was one of poverty and humiliation. He

had nowhere to lay His head, and when He died His body was laid even in a borrowed tomb.

He was rejected and despised by the people among whom He labored. "He came to that which was his own, but his own did not receive him" (John 1:11). His work was, humanly speaking, a complete failure. When He left the world, He had but a handful of followers who had remained true to His teachings and person.

His very friends and companions were of the humblest class, rude fishermen and common people without culture and, indeed, often without the ability to appreciate their blessed Master. Coming from the society of heaven, how He must have felt the strange difference of these rude associates; and yet, never once did He complain or even intimate the difference.

The spirit of His life was ever chastened and humble. The veil of modesty covered all His acts and attitudes. He never boasted or vaunted Himself. "He will not quarrel or cry out; no one will hear his voice in the streets" (Matthew 12:19) was the prophetic picture which He so literally fulfilled. He sought no splendid pageants, asked no earthly honors; and the only time that He did assume the prerogatives of a king, He rode upon the foal of an ass and entered Jerusalem in triumph as the King of meekness rather than of pride.

Perhaps the severest strain of all His life was the repression of Himself. Knowing that He was Almighty and Divine, He yet held back the exercise of His supernatural powers. Knowing that with one withering glance he could have stricken His enemies and laid them lifeless at His feet, He restrained His power. Knowing that He could have summoned all the angels of heaven to His defense, He surrendered Himself to His captors in helplessness and defenselessness. He even surrendered the exercise of His own will and drew from His Heavenly Father the very grace and power which He needed from day to day, the same as any sinful man who lives by faith and prayer. "By myself I can do nothing" (John 5:30), He said. "Just as the living Father sent me and I live because of the Father, so the one who feeds on me will live because of me" (6:57). He took the same place of dependence that the humblest believer takes today, and in all things lived a life of self-renunciation.

At last the climax came to the supreme trial of the judgment hall and the cruel cross. When He became obedient unto death, a death of shame and unparalleled humiliations, insults and agonies completed His life sacrifices for the salvation of His people. What words can ever describe, what tongue can ever tell the weight, the sharpness, the agony of that cruel cross, the fierceness of His fight with the powers of darkness, and the depths of woe when even His Father's face was averted and He bore for us the hell that sin deserved.

After His resurrection, He still bore the marks of the cross. The few glimpses that we find of the risen Christ are all marked by the same touches of gentleness, self-abnegation and remembered suffering. The very evidences that He gave them that He was the same Jesus were the marks of the spear and the nails. And in His manifestations to them, especially in that memorable scene at Emmaus, we see the same gentle, unobtrusive Christ, walking with them by the way unrecognized, and then quietly vanishing out of their sight when at last they knew Him.

And even on the throne to which He has now ascended, the same cross marks still remain amid the glories of the heavenly world. John beheld Him as "a Lamb looking as if it had been slain" (Revelation 5:6). The Christ of heaven still bears the old marks of the cross as His highest glory and His everlasting memorial. Such are the marks of the Lord Jesus. And all who claim to be His followers and His ministers may well imitate them. The men who claim to be His apostles and ambassadors, and who come to us with the sound of trumpets, the bluster of earthly pageants and the pompous and egotistical boastings of pride and vainglory, are false prophets and wretched counterfeits of the Christ of Calvary. They can deceive only the blind and ignorant dupes who know nothing of the real Christ.

These were the marks of the Master, and they will be worn by His servants, too.

The Cross Marks of the Christian

"No servant is greater than his master" (John 13:16). The tests of the Master must be applied to His followers. We may not preach a crucified Savior without being also crucified men and women. It is not enough to wear an ornamental cross as a pretty decoration. The cross that Paul speaks about was burned into his very flesh, was branded into his being, and only the Holy Spirit can burn the true cross into our innermost life.

We are saved by identification with Christ in His death. We are justified because we have already died with Him and have thus been made free from sin. God does not whitewash people when He saves them. He has really visited their sins upon their great Substitute, the Lord Jesus Christ. Every believer was counted as in Him when He died, and so His death is our death. It puts us in the same position before the law of the supreme Judge as if we had already been executed and punished for our own guilt, as if the judgment for us was already past. Therefore, it is true of every believer, "whoever hears my word and believes him who sent me has eternal life and will not be condemned; he has crossed over from death to life" (5:24). The cross, therefore, is the very standpoint of the believer's salvation, and we shall never cease to echo the song of heaven: "Worthy is the Lamb who was slain, to receive . . . honor and glory and praise" (Revelation 5:12).

We are sanctified by dying with Christ to sin. When He hung on Calvary, He not only made a settlement for our sinful self, by faith we reckon ourselves as actually crucified with Him there to the whole life of sin. It is our privilege, therefore, to identify ourselves with Christ in His death so fully that we may lay over our sinful nature upon Him and utterly die to it, and then receive from Him a life all new, divine and pure. Henceforth we may say, "I no longer live, but Christ lives in me" (Galatians 2:20). Sanctification is not the cleansing of the old life, but the crucifying of that life and substituting for it the very life of Christ Himself, the holy and perfect One.

We must keep sanctified by dead reckoning. And dead reckoning is just the reckoning of ourselves as "dead to sin, but alive to God in Christ Jesus" (Romans 6:11). This is not merely a feeling or experience, but a counting upon Him as life and drawing from Him as breath from the air around us.

Our spiritual life is perfected by the constant recognition of the cross and by our unceasing application of it to all our life and being. We must live by the cross and must pass from death to death and life to life by constant fellowship with His sufferings and conformity unto His death, until at last we shall "attain to the resurrection from the dead" (Philippians 3:11).

Now this principle of death and resurrection underlies all nature as well as the Bible. The autumn leaves with their rich crimson are just a parable of nature's dying to make way for the resurrection of the coming spring. Pick up an acorn in the forest, and in its heart, as you break the shell, you will find a crimson hairline as the cross mark of its hidden life. When it bursts

through the ground in the spring, the first opening leaf is red, the color of the cross, and when
the leaf dies and falls in autumn, it wraps itself in
the same crimson hue.

But all this is but a steppingstone of the life that
follows. Look at the structure and growth of a
flower. First, the calyx or flower cup tightly claps
the enfolding petals, refusing to let go. But
gradually these fingers relax, these folds unclasp
and the petals burst open in all their fragrance
and beauty. But still the calyx holds them tightly
as if it would never let go, but hour by hour, as
the flower-life advances, those petals have to be
relinquished from the grasp; and in a little while
the blossom floats away on the summer winds
and seems to perish. "The flowers fall" (Isaiah
40:7), the beauty of nature dies. But observe that
after death comes a richer life. Behind the flower
you will notice a seed pod. It also is held for a
time by the grasp of another cup. But as the seeds
ripen, even they must let go this grasp, and
gradually the seed pod relaxes and at length
bursts open and the seeds are scattered and sink
into the ground and die. But from the buried seed
comes forth a new resurrection of plants and
trees and flowers and fruits. The whole process is
one of dying and living, one life giving place to a
higher, and all moving steadily on to the
reproduction of the plant and the stage of fruit
bearing.

So marked is this principle in the natural world
that botanists tell us that when a flower gives too

much attention to the blossom and develops into a double flower, which is the most beautiful form of the blossom, it becomes barren and fruitless. Nature puts its ban upon self life even in a flower. It must die and pass away if it would bear much fruit. A beautiful double petunia is no good; but a single-petalled blossom has in it the life of another generation. And so our spiritual life must pass down to deeper deaths and on and up to the higher experiences of life, or we shall lose even what we have. We cannot cling to the sweetest spiritual experiences, the fondest object of our highest joy, without ceasing to grow and ceasing to bear that fruit which is the very nature of our salvation.

The Principle of Death in Our Deeper Life

We must learn not only to give up our wrongs, but even our rights. It is little that we should turn from sin; if we are to follow Christ and His consecration, we must turn from the things that are not sinful and learn the great lesson of self-renunciation even in rightful things. The everlasting ideal is He, in the form of God, who thought it not a thing to be eagerly grasped that He should be equal with God, but emptied Himself and became obedient unto death, even the death of the cross (see Philippians 2:6–8). There are many things which are not wrong for you to keep and to hold as your own, but in keeping them, He would lose and you would lose much more.

We have the cross mark upon our affections and friendships. Thus Abraham gave up his Isaac, and received him back with a new touch of love as God's Isaac. We shall find that most of the lives that counted much for God had somewhere in them a great renunciation, where the dearest idol was laid upon Moriah's altar and from that hour there was new fruit and power.

Our prayers must often have the mark of the cross upon them. We ask and we receive the promise and assurance of the answer; and then we must often see that answer apparently buried and forgotten, and long after come forth, to our amazement and surprise, multiplied with blessings that have grown out of the very delay and seeming denial.

So the life of our body which we may claim from Him must be marked with the cross. It is only after the strength of nature fails us that the strength of God can come in. Even then the answer is sometimes not given until we have first surrendered it to Him and have been willing to give up even life itself and have learned to seek the Blesser rather than the blessing. Then God often reveals Himself to us as a Healer, as He could not do until we were wholly abandoned to His will.

Our religious experiences must have the mark of the cross upon them. We must not cling even to our peace and joy and spiritual comfort. Sometimes, the flower must fade that the fruit may be more abundant, and that we may learn to walk by faith and not by sight.

Our service for God often must be buried before it can bring forth much fruit. And so God sometimes calls us to a work and makes it appear to fail in its early stages, until we cry in discouragement, "I have labored in vain, I have spent my strength for nought." Then it comes forth Phoenix-like from the flames, and blossoms and buds until it fills the face of the world with fruit. So God writes the mark of the cross on everything, until, by and by, the very grave may be the passport to a better resurrection, and death will be swallowed up in victory. In fact, we believe that the universe itself has yet to pass through its dissolution and come forth in the glory of a final resurrection so that the marks of the Lord Jesus may, at last, be written upon the very earth and heaven, and so that the universe to its furthest bound may reecho the great redemption song: "Worthy is the Lamb that was slain."

Beloved, have you the marks of the Lord Jesus? These sacrifices to which He sometimes calls us are just great investments that He is asking us to make and that He will refund to us with accumulated interest in the age to come.

Good Richard Cecil once asked his little daughter, as she sat upon his knee with a cluster of pretty glass beads around her neck, if she truly loved him, and if she loved him enough to take those beads and fling them into the fire. She looked in his face with wonder and grief; she could hardly believe that he meant such sacrifice.

But his steady gaze convinced her that he was in earnest; and with trembling, reluctant steps she tottered to the grate, and clinging to them with reluctant fingers, at last dropped them into the fire, and then flinging herself into his arms, she sobbed herself to stillness in the bewilderment and perplexity of her renunciation. He let her learn her lesson fully, but a few days later, on her birthday, she found upon her dressing case a little package, and on opening it she found inside a cluster of real pearls strung upon a necklace and bearing her name with her father's love. She had scarcely time to grasp the beautiful present as she flew to his presence and throwing herself in his arms, she said, "Oh, Papa, I am so sorry that I did not understand."

Some day, beloved, in His arms, you will understand. He does not always explain it now. He lets the cross have all its sharpness. He lets the weary years go by; but oh, some day we will understand and be so glad that we were permitted to bear with Him and for Him the "brand marks of the Lord Jesus."

The Uplift of the Cross

But I, when I am lifted up from the earth,
will draw all men to myself. (John 12:32)

Astory is told of a medieval saint who asked his attendants to lift him from his death bed and place him on a cross. As he lay there and breathed out his life, he kept repeating with glowing eye and shining face the simple words, "It lifts me up; it lifts me up." These words suggest the uplifting power of the cross of Jesus Christ. That which naturally suggests only suffering, ignominy and defeat has become the noblest sign of all that is lofty, heroic and glorious in the story of redemption and the experience of the Christian.

The Uplift of the Cross in the Experience of the Lord Jesus Christ Himself

Speaking of it, He said, "I, when I am lifted up

from the earth" (12:32). To Him it brought no sense of degradation or of failure, but only a sense of glory and honor and victory. As He spoke of it to His disciples in advance, it was always only as a steppingstone to the resurrection which was to follow. On the Mount of Transfiguration His heavenly visitors conversed of nothing else, but they spoke of it as "his decease (departure, NIV) which he should accomplish at Jerusalem" (Luke 9:31, KJV), and the word "decease" expresses not so much the idea of death as of departure. It was but the beginning of a glorious ascension which was to lift Him up to higher honors and loftier ministries through the ages to come.

The Apostle Paul, speaking of the cross, can express himself only in terms of the loftiest exultation, "May I never boast except in the cross of our Lord Jesus Christ" (Galatians 6:14). In the visions of the Apocalypse we find it occupying the place of highest honor in the heavenly world. It is the continual theme of the songs, both of the angels and the ransomed. The highest distinction of Him who shares the Father's throne is the mark of the cross. He is described as the "Lamb looking as if it had been slain" (Revelation 5:6).

The cross of Jesus Christ has exalted Christ Himself by giving to the universe a manifestation not only of the wisdom and love of God nowhere else found, but especially a manifestation of the self-sacrificing love of Christ Himself transcending all other revelations of His character and glory. In human history there is something higher than wealth, power or brilliant gifts of intellect. Grecian history commemorates the heroes of Thermopylae above all the other records of their country. Rome gloried in the legend of Horatius far more than in the pomp and pageantry of Augustus and Hadrian. The fame of Lincoln and McKinley has been heightened by the tragic story of their martyrdom. And the annuals of Christian biography are rich in the record of heroic sacrifice. But there is no heroism like the story of Calvary, and there is no glory which shall ever be laid at the feet of the Lamb of God to be compared with the crimson of the cross and the crown of thorns.

But the cross has brought to the Lord Jesus Christ a yet higher recompense in the approval of His Father and the love of His people. What human imagination can conceive the rapture of that hour, when at last He rested on His Father's bosom, after the anguish of the garden and the crucifixion and the awful descent among the dead. Speaking of the Father's recompense, the inspired apostle says, "Therefore God exalted him to the highest place and gave him the name that is above every name" (Philippians 2:9). Almost as sweet to His heart is the devotion of His people and the love and gratitude of those for whom He died. How much a brave man will often dare for the object of his affection, and there is no reward so sweet to him as the thanks of someone dear to his heart whom he has been permitted to help or save.

When we think of the myriads whom Jesus Christ has rescued from sin and despair, we can form some conception of the meaning of that promise, "He will see the light of life and be satisfied" (Isaiah 53:11). As we think of the beautiful lives that we have known, the Christians we have met, the saints we have seen pass through the gates with robes made white in the blood of the Lamb, doubtless we have often felt that for such it would not be too much even for us to die. This was "the joy set before him" for which He "endured the cross, scorning its shame, and sat down at the right hand of the throne of God" (Hebrews 12:2). The day is coming which will make up for all His shame and sorrow, when He will present to Himself His glorious bride, "without stain or wrinkle, or any other blemish" (Ephesians 5:27), and He will be satisfied.

The cross has brought to Christ a glorious and everlasting kingdom. The throne which the Father has prepared for Him as our Mediatorial King is a far more glorious throne than that of Deity. The kingdom which the coming ages is to bring is the recompense which He has won through the work of redemption; and the scepter, which He is to wield over the millennial world and the new heavens and earth, is one which He could never have possessed but for the sharpness of the cross and the humiliation of Bethlehem and Calvary. Therefore, it is indeed true the cross has lifted up the Son of man as well as all who follow him in that pathway of suffering and glory.

The Uplift of the Cross in the Believer's Life

It lifts us up from hell to heaven, from the curse of the broken law to the acceptance of God and the justification, forgiveness and salvation which place us on a plane of loftier righteousness than even if we had never sinned.

It lifts us up from sin to righteousness, from the degradation and defilement of our natural condition to the image of Christ and the righteousness of God. "To him who loves us and has freed us from our sins by his blood" (Revelation 1:5) is the tribute which every saint has brought to the cross of Jesus Christ. Not only does it save, it also sanctifies. But it sanctifies in a way which lifts us higher than any holiness that Adam ever knew. It sanctifies us by the process of crucifixion and resurrection. It puts not only our past sins, but our sinful nature on the cross with Jesus Christ, so that we pass out in our own sinfulness and are reckoned dead, and then in Christ Jesus we are resurrected and filled with His nature and spirit, so that we become partakers of His holiness and stand in the same place as Christ Himself in spotless holiness and blamelessness before the throne of God.

The cross lifts us above our sickness and infirmity and makes us partakers of the resurrection life and strength of the Lord Jesus even in our mortal frame, for "He took up our infirmities and carried our diseases" (Matthew 8:17) and "by his

wounds you have been healed" (1 Peter 2:24).
This is but the beginning of a physical immortality which is yet to transform us into the likeness of His glorified body and the possession of
physical attributes and qualities infinitely grander
than the race of Adam could ever have known,
but for the work of redemption.

The cross lifts us up above the world's ambitions and sordid interests and makes us the
citizens of heaven. This was the supreme reason
why Paul gloried in the cross. "Through which,"
he says, "the world has been crucified to me, and
I to the world" (Galatians 6:14), and had been
sent back to it from heaven as divine messengers
and missionaries in the very same sense as Christ
Himself was sent. The world's pleasures and pur-
suits, therefore, have no right to control us. We
are not of it any more than He was of it, and we
are in it as men who walk with our feet on earth
and our hearts and heads in heaven.

It lifts us up above the power of Satan and
makes us conquerors in the conflict with the
powers of darkness. "They overcame him by the
blood of the Lamb" (Revelation 12:11). The cross
was Satan's Waterloo. Not only was he beaten
there, but he was captured and hung up on the
cross as a scarecrow to show the children of God
that the devil is a defeated foe, and that we need
no longer fear him or even fight him in our own
name and strength; but we may hand him over to
the Captain of our salvation, who has conquered
him for us and will conquer him in us when we

fully trust Him. "Having disarmed the powers and authorities, he made a public spectacle of them, triumphing over them by *the cross*" (Colossians 2:15, italics added).

The cross lifts us above the fear of death and gives to us the right to the resurrection and the life immortal. Indeed, it is our privilege to regard death as already behind us. With Him we have died on the cross, and for us, death never can be the same again. The form of death may come, but all that has death in it has already passed upon Him; for us it is but a transition to the life beyond. "If anyone keeps my word," He has told us, "he will never see death" (John 8:51). All he shall see is the presence of the Lord encompassing him and hiding from him all other consciousness and every fear and every foe. From the standpoint of the cross we are not now looking into the grave but into the heavens "and we eagerly await a Savior from there, the Lord Jesus Christ, who, by the power that enables him to bring everything under his control, will transform our lowly bodies so that they will be like his glorious body" (Philippians 3:20–21).

The cross lifts us above the natural to the supernatural, from the human to the divine, from the Adamic race to the family of God where we are joint heirs with Jesus Christ and sons of God. Henceforth we live not according to the limitations of human nature, but by that "which he exerted in Christ when he raised him from the dead and seated him at his right hand in the heavenly

realms, far above all rule and authority, power
and dominion, and every title that can be given,
not only in the present age but also in the one to
come" (Ephesians 1:20–21).

The cross lifts us up from law to grace, from
trying to trusting, from having to, to loving to,
from our deadly doing to His finished work, from
Christian endeavor to divine achievement and victorious all-sufficiency. Henceforth it is not what
we are to do, but what we are to receive and let
Him work in us "to will and to act according to his
good purpose" (Philippians 2:13).

The cross lifts us up from the life of repression
and depression to the life of inspiration, liberty,
spontaneity and fullness. Henceforth we are not
everlastingly dying, but we have died and are alive
forevermore. The cross has taken us across the
dark abyss of death and planted us forever on the
shores of life for "Christ Jesus, who has destroyed
death and has brought life and immortality to
light through the gospel" (2 Timothy 1:10).

The cross lifts us up from a life of selfishness to a
life of sacrifice and love. Its message is: "For
Christ's love compels us, because we are convinced
that one died for all, and therefore all died. And he
died for all, that those who live should no longer
live for themselves but for him who died for them
and was raised again" (2 Corinthians 5:14–15). No
spirit that truly touches the cross can ever henceforth live for self alone. The law of the cross is the
law of sacrifice.

There is a school of religious teachers who hold

and teach that the one meaning of the cross is simply a pattern of divine love given to us for our imitation. According to this view Christ died to lift men from ignoble selfishness to heroic sacrifice and holy service. They see no place for the doctrine of substitution and atonement for sin, but see only a splendid object lesson of benevolence and sacrifice. It must be said that oftentimes the lives of the men and women who hold this lower view of the cross are by no means inconsistent with their teaching, and that they have given many beautiful examples of the loveliest virtues and the loftiest benevolence. Surely while we believe in the loftier conception of the cross of Jesus we should not leave out the lower, and our lives should show a still higher conformity to the gospel we preach and be no less noble, self-denying and beneficent than the lives of men and women who have no such inspiration as comes to us from the Source of our redemption. Perhaps it may be said for them, that believing as they do not so much in grace as in gracious works on their own part, they make more strenuous efforts to live their religion, but surely love and gratitude should win from us a nobler response than mere self righteousness from others.

While we accept His grace and praise Him for His precious blood, oh, let us not forget to follow in His blood-marked steps, and to live as well as sing,

    Cross of Christ lead onward
      in this holy war:
    In this sign we conquer
      now and evermore.

The Believer's Attitude toward the Cross

In conclusion, what is our attitude toward the cross of Christ? Near the cross? No, that will never do. At the cross? No, that is not yet near enough. On the Cross? That is our true place. Our sins on the cross? No, our very selves upon the cross. But we must not linger on the cross forever. There is another stage. In the fifteenth chapter of First Corinthians, the apostle declared, "Christ died for our sins according to the Scriptures, [and] was buried" (1 Corinthians 15:3). Too often we forget this part. This is not on the cross, but beneath the cross and beyond the cross. Like Him we are to pass from the cross to the grave. Burial with Him in baptism is the Christian symbol of this glorious fact that the cross of Christ has finished for us the question of our death with Him and has brought us to the place of resurrection and life forevermore. Is that our place? Are we reckoning ourselves dead indeed unto sin, but alive unto God through Jesus Christ our Lord?

Finally, let us not forget to take up our cross and follow Him, and inject the spirit of the cross, which is the spirit of sacrifice, of service and self-forgetting love, into everything we think and say and do. "And he died for all, that those who live should no longer live for themselves but for him who died for them and was raised again" (2 Corinthians 5:15).

Enemies of the Cross

Many live as the enemies of the cross of Christ. (Philippians 3:18)

They are crucifying the Son of God all over again. (Hebrews 6:6)

Once more we stand facing the cross of Jesus Christ, that wondrous cross which is at once the measure of the love of heaven and the sin of man. For as the cross represents the supreme act and evidence of the love of God, even so our attitude toward it represents for us the greatest blessing or the greatest sin. It is still true, as of old, "one on each side and Jesus in the middle" (John 19:18). That central cross divides the world into the saved and the lost, the heirs of glory and the children of wrath.

Something like this must have been in the mind

of the author of the Epistle to the Hebrews when he penned that dismal sentence, "They are crucifying the Son of God all over again and subjecting him to public disgrace" (Hebrews 6:6). All that he meant by that awful word of warning may be difficult to define, yet it is wise to trace those steps that may lead someday to that dreadful place where the very cross that was meant to save, can only become "the smell of death" (2 Corinthians 2:16).

It is possible to be among the enemies of the cross of Christ long before we have reached that final state and "[crucify] the Son of God all over again and [subject] him to public disgrace" (Hebrews 6:6).

Ignoring or Depreciating the Doctrine

We may take the wrong side of the cross of Christ by ignoring or depreciating the doctrine of the cross. The very foundation of Christianity is the gospel of the cross. Take that away and we have nothing left but a scheme of philosophy and morals. But alas, in the craze for novelty, religious leaders are growing weary of the old story, and they invent a new doctrine of the cross. They tell us that Jesus Christ died not to atone for the sins of men or to bear our guilt and stand beneath the judgment of God as our Substitute and Sacrifice for sin, but simply that He might inspire other men to live a similar life of sacrifice for their fellows. The atonement, according to these wild weavers of the spider's webs of the

New Theology, is simply learning to imitate the self-sacrifice of the Lord Jesus and, like Him, give our lives for our fellowmen. Is it too much to say that such a caricature of Calvary and Christianity "[crucifies] the Son of God all over again and [subjects] him to public disgrace" (Hebrews 6:6)?

Believing False Doctrine

We may also take the wrong side of the cross by believing false doctrine respecting the cross and the precious blood. The Roman Catholic sacrifice of the mass is a fearful misrepresentation of the cross of Christ. In that man-made ceremony, the Lord Jesus is represented as really offered again in actual sacrifice every time the worshiper receives the sacrament. It is literally crucifying Him afresh. In distinction from this, how emphatic is the teaching of the Epistle to the Hebrews, that "once at the end of the ages," or better, "he has appeared once for all . . . to do away with sin by the sacrifice of himself" (Hebrews 9:26).

Neglecting to Give Due Emphasis to the Doctrine

We may be enemies of the cross by neglecting to give due emphasis and importance to the doctrine of the cross and the blood of Christ. This charge holds against much of the preaching of today. As the expression goes, all roads lead to Rome, so all truths point to Calvary, and there is probably no gospel message in which the cross of

Christ should not find some place. And yet, in answer to a challenge from a brother minister, I once searched through volume after volume of published sermons of one of the greatest preachers of modern times in a vain endeavor to find one single mention of the atoning blood.

Doubting the Efficacy of the Blood

We may also be enemies of the cross by accepting the gospel and yet doubting the efficacy of the blood of Christ for our salvation and our sins. After you have laid your sins upon that cross with your crucified Savior, you have no business ever to touch them again. You honor the blood of Christ by simply and fully believing that the Lamb of God takes away the sins of the world and your sins also. When you go back and dig up your buried bones, you are really crucifying Christ afresh, and it is no wonder that your soul is poisoned and your spiritual health destroyed by the resurrection of your buried sins. You are really crucifying Christ afresh when you put back on Him the sins which have once been confessed and cleansed by His precious blood. Therefore, doubting is a dangerous and almost fatal sin. "We have come to share in Christ if we hold firmly till the end the confidence we had at first" (Hebrews 3:14).

Failing to Claim and Receive
the Full Purchase

We may be on the wrong side of the cross by

failing to claim and receive the full purchase of His blood and the full meaning and value of the cross. That blood was too sacred and costly for us to waste, and we have no right to let one drop of it be shed in vain. Not only did He die that our sins might be forgiven, but that our souls might be cleansed and sanctified. "By one sacrifice he has made perfect forever those who are being made holy" (Hebrews 10:14). "The blood of Jesus, his Son, purifies us from all sin" (1 John 1:7). If, therefore, we fail to enter into our full inheritance of grace and holiness, we are dishonoring the cross and suffering Him to die in vain.

That cross embraces our healing, also, "Surely he took up our infirmities and carried our sorrows, . . . and by his wounds we are healed" (Isaiah 53:4–5). When we fail to claim our physical redemption through Christ's atonement, we dishonor His cross to that extent. And when we take our full redemption for soul and body in His name and through the purchase of His blood, we honor the Son of God and exalt the glory of the cross before both earth and heaven. By that precious blood and that mighty cross, He has purchased for us all our redemption rights and all our inheritance of spiritual blessing. By virtue of it we have access to God in prayer and may ask according to the full measure of the value of the precious blood. Are we entering into this full inheritance, or are we coming short of anything which He died to purchase for us?

Cherishing an Unforgiving Spirit

We may also be enemies by cherishing an un-
forgiving spirit toward those whom God has forgiven and for whom Christ died. Do you realize
that when you harbor a spirit of resentment
against your brother and dwell bitterly upon his
faults and sins, that those very sins have already
been borne by his Redeemer and yours upon the
cross, and that God is saying to you, "Who will
bring any charge against those whom God has
chosen? It is God who justifies. Who is he that
condemns? Christ Jesus who died" (Romans
8:33–34). You are really crucifying Christ afresh
by taking your brother's sins off that cross and
putting them back on Him again. How dare you
thus dishonor and insult the blood to which you
owe your own salvation?

Claiming Salvation and Continuing in Sin

By claiming salvation through the blood of
Christ and yet continuing in sin, we also prove
ourselves to be enemies of the cross. If Christ has
borne your sins, you have no right to lay them
upon Him again by continuing in the same
course from which He saved you at such tremendous cost. All willful sin is a crucifying of Christ
afresh and a denying of the blood that bought
you. The little child expressed the true spirit of
the cross when she said, "Yes, I have laid my sins
on Jesus, but God helping me, I do not want to
lay any more on Him." "Shall we go on sinning

so that grace may increase? By no means! We died to sin; how can we live in it any longer?" (6:1–2). Do you expect the Lamb of God to come back and be crucified again for the sins you are presumptuously allowing? There is infinite room in the mercy of God and the blood of Christ for our frailties and our shortcomings, but the soul that persistently and willfully continues in any known course of evil is insulting the name of Jesus and is running close to the tremendous warning of this solemn text.

Giving Place to the Devil

By giving place to the devil and failing to treat him as a conquered foe, we are enemies of Christ's cross. The testimony of the Holy Spirit in the New Testament to the cross of Jesus is that by the cross Satan has been disarmed, and now we may meet him as a conquered foe. "And having disarmed the powers and authorities, he made a public spectacle of them, triumphing over them by the cross" (Colossians 2:15). Satan's weapons have been hung up in derision on the cross of Calvary, and Satan himself has been put on exhibition there, like the brazen serpent of old, as a mere empty, fangless thing. He is as powerless to harm as that metal figure hung up in the wilderness of Sinai, as a parody and mocker of his boasted power. Are you thus treating your spiritual enemy in the light of the cross of Calvary, or are you letting the mighty victory of the Captain of your salvation go for nought?

Shunning the Crosses We Share with Jesus

By shunning the crosses that God permits us to share with Jesus we show that we are enemies of the cross. For His cross means our cross too, the fellowship of His sufferings and the partnership of His burdens. If we believe He bore our cross, we will be glad to share His and "rejoice that [we] participate in the sufferings of Christ, so that [we] may be overjoyed when his glory is revealed" (1 Peter 4:13). It will make an infinite difference in the trials of life if we will learn to accept them from the hands of Jesus as tokens of His confidence and love and of our fellowship with Him in His burdens. And when we rebel at our hard fortune, shun our cross and seek for a life of self-indulgence, we are really crucifying the Son of God afresh. While He has borne all that is necessary for our salvation, He has left behind some suffering for each of His disciples, and if we refuse to take our share, we virtually declare that we are willing to crucify Him afresh and to make Him bear a second cross instead of us.

Failing to Share the Gospel

Finally, we are enemies of the cross when we fail to share the gospel and lift up the cross to all our fellowmen. For there is for our blessed Lord a greater anguish than even that bitter cross; namely, the sorrow of dying in vain for some of those precious souls who have never yet heard the story of His love. His part was to bear their cross, but our part is to tell them the story of His love and bring them to share the joy of His salvation. It is thus that He shall "see of the travail of his soul, and shall be satisfied" (Isaiah 53:11, KJV). If we are denying Him this satisfaction, we are laying upon his heart a far heavier burden than they laid in that tragic day eighteen hundred years ago, when they compelled Him to bear His cross, and they pierced His hands and feet and brow and side with the cruel nails and thorns and spear.

Beloved, this vision was the sublime joy that gave Him strength to endure the cross and despise the shame, even the vision that came to Him just as He was marching down that valley of the shadow of death, that vision that led Him to cry, "Now is the Son of Man glorified" (John 13:31), and "I, when I am lifted up from the earth, will draw all men to myself" (12:32).

Oh, are you and I holding back any part of that joy from the Master's heart? Are we selfishly hoarding this great salvation, and absorbed in the cares and ambitions of earth, scarcely lifting a hand or sacrificing a single indulgence to send the gospel to those perishing millions who are like fields white to harvest and whom God's providence has placed within our reach by the most extraordinary opportunity that any age or generation ever saw? God save us from the guilt and danger by this awful neglect of crucifying the Son of God afresh and being found enemies of the cross of Christ.

Under an Eastern sky,
Amid a rabble cry,
A Man went forth to die
    For me.

Thorn-crowned His blessed head,
Blood-stained his weary tread,
Cross-laden He was led
    For me.

Pierced were His hands and feet,
Three hours upon Him beat
Fierce rays of noontide heat
    For me.

Thus wert Thou made all mine;
Lord, make me wholly Thine,
Grant grace and strength divine
    For me.

In thought and word and deed
Thy will to do; O lead
My soul, e'en though it bleed,
    To Thee.

It goes without saying that these are the enemies of the cross of Christ who reject the Lord Jesus and permit Him, as far as they are concerned, to die in vain. The awfulness of that sin is one of the lurid messages of the Epistle to the Hebrews: "How shall we escape," the writer asks, "if we ignore such a great salvation?"

(Hebrews 2:3). In another place he speaks of the sinner who, turning away from the Lord Jesus, has "trampled the Son of God under foot, who has treated as an unholy thing the blood of the covenant that sanctified him, and who has insulted the Spirit of grace" (Hebrews 10:29).

I have read of a man rushing madly to suicide over the body of a loving wife who vainly sought to hold him back and who shrank beneath his violence as he rushed to his destruction over her bleeding body. Oh, sinner, if you reject the Son of God and if you dare face eternity without having definitely accepted the bleeding body of the Son of God, you are staining your willful feet with His precious blood. No other sin can damn your soul. "Whoever does not believe stands condemned already because he has not believed in the name of God's one and only Son" (John 3:18). Still it is true that central cross divides the world. "One on each side and Jesus in the middle" (19:18). Be sure you are not on the wrong side of the cross.

> Two souls went forth from the cross
>   that day,
>   Both dying by Jesus' side.
> On either side with the Lord between,
>   But apart how far and wide?
>
> For one went out into endless night,
>   Heaven open before his eyes,
> And one went in with the Son of God

Through the gates of Paradise.

Two souls will go from this place today,
  Both children of guilt and sin,
But one has said "no" to the Son of
      God,
  The other has let Him in.

And bright as the light of love and
      heaven,
  Redeemed one, thy path shall be.
But the gloom and the doom of endless
      night,
  Poor lost one await for thee.

The Cross and the World

If any household is too small for a whole lamb, they must share one with their nearest neighbor, having taken into account the number of people there are. (Exodus 12:4)

The Paschal lamb was God's special type of Jesus Christ, "the Lamb of God, who takes away the sin of the world!" (John 1:29). The lamb selected for the Hebrew Passover was kept apart until the fourth day so that all might have an opportunity of inspecting its perfect blamelessness; and then it was slain and its blood sprinkled upon the doorframes, and the flesh eaten by the household. So Jesus Christ, the Lamb of God, was set apart and manifested to all the people for three and a half years, that all might see that He was "holy, blameless, pure, set apart from sinners" (Hebrews 7:26). Then in the fourth year He too was slain for the sins of men, and His life became the Living Bread of all households of faith.

Jesus, the Lamb of God

God's most precious gift to us lost and sinful men was the Lamb of God. As we realize the curse of sin—and each of us has sometimes felt the dreadfulness of a sense of guilt and condemnation—and then look upon the sprinkled blood and hear God say, "When I see the blood, I will pass over you" (Exodus 12:13), we must feel that among all precious things there is nothing like "the precious blood of Christ, a lamb without blemish or defect" (1 Peter 1:19). And as we realize our weakness and step out on our pilgrim path through the desert of life, it is even more precious to feed upon His very life and echo back His own gracious word, "For my flesh is real food and my blood is real drink" (John 6:55). The old redemption song may have lost its charm for an age of higher criticism and self-sufficient humanitarianism, but for us the sweetest note in earth and heaven shall ever be:

> Dear, dying Lamb, Thy precious blood
> Shall never lose its power,
> Till all the ransomed Church of God,
> Be saved to sin no more.

Fellowship and Family Sacrifice

It was one of the provisions of the Passover Law that no man could eat his passover alone. It was a fellowship and family sacrifice. Together the household sat down and looked up at the doorframe dripping with the sprinkled blood, with a sense of infinite safety, and then together partook of the flesh of the lamb. So the sacrifice of Jesus Christ can never be an object of selfishness or a monopoly of the few. Men can monopolize many earthly honors and treasures, but the blood of Jesus Christ belongs to all our sinful race.

No doubt the household suggests the family. From the beginning God has included the home circle in the covenant of redemption. He recognizes the tender and sacred ties that bind us to our loved ones, and the promise is to us and to our children, "Believe in the Lord Jesus, and you will be saved—you and your household" (Acts 16:31). One of the sweetest joys we have is the joy of praying for the salvation of our homes and thanking God for children in the household of faith. And one of the saddest shadows that has rested upon our hearts has been to think of the blighted homes and lost lambs of the heathen world where the gospel has never been known. If ever you have had to part at the graveside with a beloved child, saved perhaps from great sin in answer to your prayers through the precious blood of Jesus Christ, I am sure your heart has

gone up to heaven with a thrill of joy and thank-
fulness even greater than for your own salvation.
You have blessed His holy name for the arms that
could reach out where yours could not have
reached and could rescue from the gulf of sin and
hell, and carry through suffering and death that
life which was dearer than your own. Thank God
for the Lamb that is sufficient for our households
as well as ourselves.

But the household has a wider meaning. It takes
in the whole household of faith and the whole
family of God. The blood of Jesus Christ has
redeemed His church and is the bond that binds
it into a greater family.

The apostle, speaking of the relation of the
church to the redemption of Christ, uses this language: "The church of God, which he bought
with his own blood" (20:28). And again we read,

> Christ loved the church and gave him-
> self up for her to make her holy, cleans-
> ing her by the washing with water
> through the word, and to present her to
> himself as a radiant church, without
> stain or wrinkle or any other blemish,
> but holy and blameless. (Ephesians
> 5:25–27)

In this sense the Lamb is for the whole
household of faith, and we together share the
redemption and a grateful song: "To him who
loves us and has freed us from our sins by his

blood, and has made us to be a kingdom and priests to serve his God and Father—to him be glory and power for ever and ever!" (Revelation 1:5–6).

But there is a wider circle than this. In this ancient appointment of the passover, God seemed to have been looking down the ages and to have anticipated the selfishness and bigotry of His earthly people, Israel, and of the spiritual church which should succeed to her privileges. "If any household is too small for a whole lamb" (Exodus 12:4), was evidently meant to remind Israel that while the Lamb of God primarily came to be their Redeemer, His message of grace was not limited to them, but He was also to be "a light for revelation to the Gentiles" as well as the "glory of [his] people Israel" (Luke 2:32). The household of Israel was too little for the Lamb of God. Even if they had accepted Him as their Messiah, they would have been led out in a larger ministry to the Gentile world for which He had also died. For us too there is the same significant hint that God will not permit us to monopolize His grace or keep His blood-bought salvation for ourselves alone. Christ is too much for what we call Christendom, and He bids us share His precious blood and His victorious life with our neighbor and our race.

The largeness of the Lamb of God, the scope of the gospel of Jesus Christ, the boundless length and breadth of divine love, the universality of the message of salvation, the right of every sinful man to hear and accept the mercy of God—this is the glorious thought that this ancient text suggests. The Bible is full of this glorious theme. "For God so loved the world that he gave his one and only Son, that whoever believes in him shall not perish but have eternal life" (John 3:16).

The mercy of heaven is big enough to take in all our sinful race. The blood of Christ is rich enough to cover the guilt of every child of Adam. The gospel is broad enough to take in whosoever will. The life of Jesus Christ is full enough to save and sanctify and keep all the myriads of our race, if they will but accept it. The heaven that He has provided is vast enough for all earth's lost generations. And the divine plan is grand enough to take in every kindred and tribe and tongue, all earth's countless inhabitants. There may be limitations in the receiving of God's grace on our part through the ignorance, willfulness or indifference of sinful men, but there is no limitation to the sufficiency of Christ's redemption and the universal and all-embracing fullness of the gospel of salvation.

Sharing the Lamb

What does all this mean for us as redeemed men and women? Surely this, that we have no right to claim the purchase of the Savior's blood for ourselves alone, and that we are guilty of selfishness, dishonesty and base ingratitude, if we can be content to be saved without having done everything in our power to give to our fellowmen an equal opportunity of eternal life. Have we lived it? Is it the spirit and purpose of our whole conduct, or are we guilty of the crime of hoarding the gospel and keeping to ourselves that great salvation which was committed to us as a sacred trust?

But who is the neighbor with whom we are to share God's Lamb? He is spoken of here as the one that is over against us, the one that is in closest contact with us. Surely, that means that God brings people into touch with us in order that we may be stewards of His grace to them. The people in your family, the servant in your household, your fellow travelers, the partners of your social and business life—these are among the neighbors to whom you owe a spiritual responsibility. Have you met it according to your utmost ability and can you truly say, "I am pure from the blood of all men"?

But that is the narrowest circle. What about that larger world of lost men and women that God has also brought into touch with His church? We must go to those who have never heard! How marvelously God has brought over against us as Christian nations the people of heathen lands as our great wards. Look at the millions of Indian tribes, scattered over this western hemisphere still in paganism. Surely, they are over against us in the most providential way. We have taken their country from them. We have driven them from their heritage. What have we given them in return?

Look at the hundreds of millions of Africans. Although brought by bitter and unchristian circumstances, eight or ten million of their children were placed in our country as hostages for this mighty race. While not to condone the actions of our forefathers, it was because of those circumstances that many heard the gospel and were saved. God has given Christian nations a mighty trusteeship by virtue of their colonial possessions, their commercial interests and their social connections and ties in that great continent. Look at the millions of the West Indies and the Philippines. Surely God has brought them over against us in His providence and created for us an inexorable responsibility, not only to give them the citizenship of earth, but of heaven also.

Look at the Hindu people. Great Britain was in the providence of God the guardian of their liberties, and her Christian people should surely be the stewards of God's richer blessings of life and salvation to these benighted and yet most gifted people. And what shall we say of China? It confronts us on the shore of the great Pacific Ocean as our nearest and mightiest neighbor. Its people have come to us as hostages for their nation. Its commerce is attracting our enterprise. Surely, its awful spiritual need and immense possibilities for God and humanity constitute a responsibility and a call which no language can adequately express. These are our neighbors in the most providential, practical and present tense way. We have given them our literature. We have given them our commerce. We have given them our civilization. We have taught them to surpass us in the arts of peace and war. Have we given them the Lamb of God, the gospel of Christ, the chief heritage of blessing that has come to us, the opportunity of eternal life through Jesus Christ, our Lord? Oh, what splendid disciples these mighty nations offer for new triumphs of the glorious gospel of Jesus Christ! What it has done for us may be duplicated and multiplied a thousand times among these teeming millions. Our household is too small a theater for all the purposes which God has intended through these new communities and nations.

There came a time in the history of apostolic missions when God pushed out His servants into the continent of Europe, because it was to be the theater for the coming centuries of the world's greatest events. So in later centuries God has still further pushed on the course of empire. Think of the immense issues that have followed the discovery of America and the opening up of this continent to modern civilization. But if God could accomplish so much with a hundred million in this land in a single century, how much more can He accomplish through the gospel with the millions in the vaster continent of Asia, who are just awaking to all the possibilities of life, progress and intellectual and spiritual power? It was the Reformation and the light of spiritual life that gave to modern Europe, and later to America, its intellectual and political revival. And it is the gospel that will kindle the Orient and lift the intellects of China, India and Japan to a plane much higher than ours, as ours is higher than the life of the dark ages of medieval Europe. A morning is dawning, a day is breaking over the earth, a time of great and glorious things of which we dimly dream. Let us rise to the mighty purpose of God, to the larger meaning of our times and to the glorious trust of setting free these mighty forces, by the salvation of Jesus Christ, until it shall teach the magnificent ideal of the thought of God and the divine plan of this lost age of time.

How shall we share our Lamb with our neighbor? First, let us recognize that God has saved us that we may save others. We are stewards, trustees of the gospel.

Next, let us use every practical opportunity to bring Christ into the lives of the people over against us in our own homes, in our social relations, in our businesses, in all the opportunities of life.

Again, let us become possessed with the full realization of the extent of God's love to men and the purpose of His grace for the race. Let us dwell upon this till our hearts become stirred and enlarged by it, and we know and share the heart of God toward lost and perishing sinners everywhere.

Then also, let us make the work of missions in some definite way the supreme business of our lives. Let us recognize it as the great trust of the Christian church today. Let us in every possible way impress upon men and women this thought of the church's responsibility for the lost world.

Let us circulate the light and educate the public opinion of our age along this line by conversation, by testimony, by literature, and by promotion in every way, every means by which God's people shall be brought to a more profound interest in this great work of our generation. Then let us identify ourselves with some definite plan of action. Let us give systematically. Let us be in touch with the work through its organizations, its missionaries, its literature, its plan. Let us count it our work and, as much as in us lies, do our best to strengthen and extend it. And above all else let it be the supreme object of our prayers. Prayer will set our own hearts on fire with missionary enthusiasm. And then prayer will kindle the same flame in other hearts and will bring actual forces and influences to work in every part of the world. It will lead men and women to give themselves in it. It will bring means from the most unexpected sources. It will send down the power of God upon the missionary field and lead to revivals, conversions, open doors and harvests of blessings in every land.

And finally, let us embrace such definite opportunities as God shall give to us for a direct personal work in this great cause. Some of us will give our children, some of us will give ourselves, and some of us, if we cannot go, will become responsible for those who can, and thus in person or by substitute will have an actual part in telling the story of salvation and spreading the gospel to the uttermost part of the earth.

CHAPTER

7

Voices of the Resurrection

That power is like the working of his mighty strength, which he exerted in Christ when he raised him from the dead.
(Ephesians 1:19–20)

The first message of the resurrection is that Christ is the Son of God, and Christianity is divine. He was "declared with power to be the Son of God by his resurrection from the dead" (Romans 1:4).

The one test which He always offered in proof of His lofty claims was that He should die and rise again. His sign was the sign of the prophet Jonah, or as He put it at another time in another figure, "Destroy this temple, and I will raise it again in three days" (John 2:19). So well did His enemies understand this challenge that they took every precaution to guard His tomb and prevent any possible stratagem on the part of His disciples to steal Him away. There was an ample guard, a great stone at the mouth of the tomb with the seal of Rome upon it, which it was treason for any man to break. But in spite of all, that Easter morning saw the tomb empty, the stone rolled away and the Lord of life again among His disciples. And "after his suffering, he showed himself to these men and gave many convincing proofs that he was alive" (Acts 1:3). For forty days He repeated the evidence of His resurrection on various occasions and to different witnesses, until even Thomas, the most incredulous of all, was compelled to confess, "My Lord and my God!" (John 20:28). Still later Saul of Tarsus, the bitter enemy of Christianity, beheld in a vision the actual form of the risen Christ, and added his testimony and the testimony of his life of sacrifice and suffering to the witnesses of the resurrection. So complete is the proof of this transcendent event that we have seen a gifted lawyer completely convinced after a life of skepticism by simply following the line of evidence which Horace Bushnell has laid out in his volume, *Nature and the Supernatural*. And this gentleman has afterwards frankly admitted that the proof of Christ's resurrection, by the ordinary rules of evidence, is sufficient to bring conviction to any unprejudiced judge or jury.

Dear friends, if you have ever been troubled or if you have friends who are troubled with skeptical questioning about the Bible and Christianity, let all the other issues go. Drop the question of Moses, Isaiah and Jonah, and settle the whole issue upon this supreme question: Did Jesus of Nazareth really die, and did He really rise again? And if you are fair and candid, you will be compelled to conclude, or to bring conviction to your doubting friend, that these are indeed "infallible proofs," and that the whole fabric of Christianity rests upon one supreme foundation, one rock of ages: "And if Christ has not been raised, our preaching is useless and so is your faith. . . . But Christ has indeed been raised from the dead, the firstfruits of those who have fallen asleep" (1 Corinthians 15:14, 20).

The Sacrifice Is Accepted

The second message of the resurrection is that the sacrifice of Calvary is accepted, the atonement is complete, and the great redemption is accomplished. That great Sufferer went down to the grave a prisoner of the law which man had broken, bearing the penalty of the whole guilt of the human race. Had He remained immured in the tomb, it would have been apparent that the debt was not discharged and the price was not sufficient, that He had sunk beneath His heroic but futile effort and had tried in vain to save our ruined race. But when we see Him come forth on the resurrection morning, with the approval of His Father, the presence of the angels of glory and the portents of nature in the rending earthquake and the opening tombs around, and afterwards ascend in supernatural power to the right hand of God and send down the Holy Spirit as the seal of His complete acceptance and ours, we know that His great task has been completed, that He has finished transgression and made an end of sin, and that:

> The great redemption is complete
> And Satan's power overthrown.

When the high priest of old on the great Day of Atonement passed in behind the curtains of the Tabernacle to bear the sins of the people and make reconciliation by blood and incense in the Holy of Holies, the people outside, in solemn suspense, waited for the tinkling of the bells that hung from the skirts of his priestly garments. This assured them that the lightning of divine judgment had not stricken him down for their sins, but that his offering was accepted and their guilt was covered by the sprinkled blood. And when at last he came forth through the parting curtains and raised his hands to pronounce the Levitical benediction upon their heads, they raised a great shout and fell upon their faces, for they knew that his offering was accepted, that his atonement sufficed and that for one year more the presence of Jehovah would lead them and the light of His countenance continue to rest upon them.

It is in direct allusion to this type that the apostle said, "When God raised up his servant, he sent him first to you to bless you by turning each of you from your wicked ways" (Acts 3:26). The same thought lies back of Paul's triumphant challenge, "Who is he that condemns? Christ Jesus, who died—more than that, who was raised to life—is at the right hand of God and is also interceding for us" (Romans 8:34).

Assures Our Justification

The third message is that the resurrection of Jesus Christ assures us of our justification. "He was delivered over to death for our sins and was raised to life for our justification" (4:25). The salvation of Jesus Christ is not a mere pardon doled out to a criminal, not a probation offered so long as we stand on our good behavior; but it is a complete justification, a divine decree of righteousness that puts us in the same position as if we had ourselves been already executed for our crimes and sins, and brought back again from the dead to live a second life free from all liability for our former transgressions as distinctly as if we had ceased to be the former personality. This is the force of the apostle's strong statement in the epistle to the Romans, "because anyone who has died has been freed from sin" (6:7). The margin is still stronger: "Is justified from sin."

The second Adam hung on Calvary that day with all His spiritual children embodied in His own suffering frame, and His death was their death and His resurrection. How shall we effect this? Must we somehow penetrate the secrets of

the skies and see if our names are written in His
book of life and if we belong to that mysterious
seed who share the death and resurrection and
righteousness of the second Adam? Nay, so marvelous is the free and universal offer of the gospel
that each of us can determine for himself his
identification with Christ. Just as Ruth, when she
learned that she had a legal right to the great
Levirate Law that gave her a claim upon her
kinsman-redeemer, modestly, yet boldly,
presented herself at his feet and pressed that
claim until it was recognized and honored, so
each of us may write our own names in the book
of life and say,

> When Jesus rose with life divine,
>   I, too, was there;
> His resurrection power is mine,
> And, as the branches and the vine,
>   His life I share.

The Cause of Sanctification

Fourth, the resurrection of Jesus Christ is the
efficient cause of our sanctification. I cannot better express this great truth than by quoting the
following paragraphs from an old and little
known volume that is worthy of permanent and
wide circulation, Marshall's *Gospel Mystery of
Sanctification.*

The end of Christ's incarnation, death and

resurrection was to prepare and form a holy nature and frame for us in Himself, to be communicated to us by union and fellowship with Him; and not to enable us to produce in ourselves the first original of such a holy nature by our own endeavors.

1. By His incarnation there was a man created in a new holy frame, after the holiness of the first Adam's frame had been marred and abolished for the first transgression; and this new frame was far more excellent than even the first Adam's was, because man was really joined to God by a close, inseparable union of the divine and human nature in one person—Christ; so that these natures had communion each with the other in their acting, and Christ was able to act in His human nature by power proper to the divine nature, wherein He was one God with the Father.

Why was it that Christ set up the fallen nature of man in such a wonderful nature of holiness in bringing it to live and act by communion with God living and acting in it? One great end was, that he might communicate this excellent frame to His seed that should by His Spirit be born of Him and be in Him as the last Adam, the quickening Spirit; that as we have borne the image of the earthly so we might bear the image of the heavenly (1 Cor. 15:45,49), in holiness here and in glory hereafter. Thus He was

born Emmanuel, God with us; because the
fulness of the Godhead with all holiness did
first dwell in Him bodily, even in His human
nature, that we might be filled with that
fulness in Him (Matt. 1:23; Col. 2:9,10).
Thus He came down from heaven as living
bread, that, as He liveth by the Father, so
those that eat Him may live by Him (John
6:51,57), by the same life of God in them
which was first in Him.

2. By His death He freed Himself from
the guilt of our sins imputed to Him, and
from all that innocent weakness of human
nature which He had borne for a time for
our sakes. And, by freeing Himself, He
prepared a freedom for us from our whole
nature condition; which is both weak as He
was, and also polluted with our guilt and sinful corruption. Thus the corrupt nature state
which is called in Scripture the 'old man,'
was crucified together with Christ, that the
body of sin might be destroyed. And it is
destroyed in us, not by any wounds which we
ourselves can give it, but by our partaking of
that freedom from it, and death unto it, that
is already wrought out for us by the death of
Christ; as is signified by our baptism,
wherein we are buried in Christ, by the application of His death to us (Rom.
6:2,3,4,10,11).

"God sending his own Son in the likeness
of sinful flesh, and for sin" (or, "by a sacrifice

for sin," as in the margin) "condemned sin in the flesh; that the righteousness of the law might be fulfilled in us, who walk not after the flesh, but after the Spirit" (Rom. 8:3,4).

Let these Scriptures be well observed, and they will sufficiently evidence that Christ died, not that we might be able to form a holy nature in ourselves, but that we might receive one ready prepared and formed in Christ for us, by union and fellowship with Him.

3. By his resurrection He took possession of spiritual life for us, as now fully procured for us, and made to be our right and property by the merit of His death, and therefore we are said to be quickened together with Christ. His resurrection was our resurrection to the life of holiness, as Adam's fall was our fall into spiritual death. And we are not ourselves the first makers and formers of our new holy nature, any more than of our original corruption, but both are formed ready for us to partake of them. And by union with Christ, we partake of that spiritual life that He took possession of for us at His resurrection, and thereby we are enabled to bring forth the fruits of it; as the Scripture showeth by the similitude of a marriage union, Romans 7:4: We are married in Him that is raised from the dead, that we might bring forth fruit unto God.

The Source of the Higher Life

The fifth message is that the resurrection of Jesus Christ is the source of that higher physical life which faith may claim in the experience of divine healing. While this blessed experience is founded on the death of Christ, it is much more closely connected with His risen life. The Man who rose on Easter morning was a physical man; the body that Thomas touched was a material organism brimming with life and energy not only sufficient for Himself but for all who touch Him and live in vital touch with Him. He belongs to us as our living Head, and as He lived upon His Father so we may live by Him.

Referring to His own physical life at a crisis time, the Apostle Paul says: "We might not rely on ourselves but on God, who raises the dead" (2 Corinthians 1:9). And again he says: "The life of Jesus [is] also . . . revealed in our body" (4:10). And yet again: "We are members of his body, of his flesh, and of his bones." (Ephesians 5:30, KJV). This is indeed a sacred mystery which few appear to comprehend or realize, but which is the true source and fountain of physical energy, health and strength to those who have dared to claim all the fullness of this complete redemption. It is an open secret which all may share, but into which we can come only by the great law of the fitness of things, and by coming so close to the Master that we can say with the beloved apostle: "That . . . which we have heard, which we have seen with our eyes, which we have looked at and our hands have touched—this we proclaim concerning the Word of life. The life appeared; we have seen it and testify to it, and we proclaim to you the eternal life, which was with the Father and has appeared to us" (1 John 1:1–2).

The Guarantee of Our Resurrection

The sixth voice is that the resurrection of Christ Jesus is the type and guarantee of our resurrection. It is impossible for us to explain or understand the physiological difference between the resurrection body of our Lord and that mortal frame that was nailed to Calvary's cross three days before. That it was the same body substantially the Scriptures have left no doubt; but that there were infinite differences is also as clear. It had been refined and glorified in some ineffable way beyond all that even the most advanced science has taught us of the possibilities of matter. It could come forth from the tomb, passing through the great stone which closed the sepulcher before the stone was rolled away. It could rise without an effort and by the sheer force of will from earth to heaven in spite of the laws of gravitation. It could pass through closed doors and become visible and invisible at will.

Something faintly approximating such higher forms of matter has been illustrated by the discoveries of science in connection with radium. At one time the atom was considered the smallest particle of matter, and an atom is so small that three hundred million of them could lie side by side and form a row less than a yard long. But radium has opened the way for the discovery that a single atom contains smaller particles known as electrons, and that these are intensely active and are ever moving about each other as the planets around the sun and flashing out at times a swift radiation into space at a tremendous velocity of more than a hundred thousand miles a second. And yet in its primal form, radium is just pitchblende or uranium, a mass of dull brown matter scarcely distinguishable from the dust of the ground. If you think of the lower form, and then of the higher, so mighty in its material ener-- gy that a flashlight from it could go round the globe four times in a second, and a few ounces of it would be sufficient to completely annihilate by explosion the greatest city in the world in a moment of time, you will get some conception of the possibilities of matter.

Apply all this to these bodies of clay which we are now carrying about with us with their burdens of infirmities and their fetters of disease, and then think of the time when transfigured, glorified and conformed to the body of His glory, we shall reach our splendid and eternal destiny. We shall sweep from star to star as thought sweeps swiftly now; we shall shine forth like the sun, and we shall share the omnipotence of Him who created the universe, and who tells us that "when he appears, we shall be like him" (3:2). These are the prospects and hopes which the resurrection of Jesus Christ has guaranteed.

Not only so, but that resurrection has established a precedent for the whole universe of God, and before the great plan shall have been accomplished the mark of the cross and the glory of the resurrection will be stamped upon the whole creation, for the day is coming when He that sits upon the throne shall say: "I am making everything new" (Revelation 21:5), and earth and heaven shall have their baptism of death and resurrection.

Its Crowning Glory

A seventh message is that the resurrection of Christ as its crowning glory gives us back Christ Himself. For a brief moment of eclipse the Son of Righteousness went out into the darkness of the grave, but with the Easter morning came a sunrise that shall nevermore decline. That glorious morning gave us back the crucified Jesus as our living and everlasting Friend, to be with us in a sense and in a fullness not possible had He continued to live as the Christ of Galilee. Then His presence was limited to a single spot and to a little group of friends. Now He says to us without restriction or limitation: "Surely I am with you always, to the very end of the age" (Matthew 28:20). His resurrection was the steppingstone to His ascension and to His high-priesthood before the throne where He ever lives to make intercession for us. And it is leading on to the greater glory of His second coming as King of kings and

Lord of all the ages.

Established a Precedent

Finally, the resurrection of Christ established a precedent for the highest things that faith and prayer can claim. One text gives this mighty measure where the apostle prays that their eyes may be illuminated to be "made known . . . the mystery of his will according to his good pleasure, which he purposed in Christ" (Ephesians 1:9). After the resurrection, nothing is too hard for God. After the rolling away of that stone, no barrier need ever stand in your way again. After the victory of the Conqueror of death, no foe need ever dismay you. Oh, let us ask and believe and expect according to the mighty power which He wrought in Christ when He raised Him from the dead.

And now, in conclusion, there are several great and mighty words which seem to stand out in raised letters over the gateway of the Easter morning. The first is *life*. It is the voice of the Spring; it is the voice of the resurrection. It is the key word to our great salvation-life. Have we received God's mighty gift—eternal life?

Another phrase is *springing life, spontaneous life*, that life which is given to the beautiful season of Spring; that life which makes the Christian life not an effort by an impulse, not a stagnant pool, but a glorious artesian well.

Another is *fullness of life*. All about us in nature are scattered in profusion the prodigal and redundant gifts of the Spring. Oh, let us realize that He who gave the sun its light, the trees their foliage and the landscape its myriad beauties that no human eyes shall ever fully trace, is able to do much more for the children of His grace. Let us enter into the fullness of His resurrection.

Another phrase is *newness of life*. Rejuvenescence, the scientists call it. And that is what we need in our spiritual experience, the freshness that will make us like Aaron's rod, ever budding, blossoming and bearing abundant fruit.

Another is *gladness, joyfulness*. This is the spirit of the resurrection morning. "All Hail!" is the message of the Risen One. "Fear not!" is His reassuring word. Oh, let us emulate the songs of the birds, the sunshine of the sky, the blossoms of the Spring, the shining faces of the angels who came to herald the resurrection!

Another is *victory*. That triumph assures all other victories and bids us go forth with the shout, "Thanks be to God, who always leads us in triumphal procession in Christ" (2 Corinthians 2:14).

One other word let us not forget. The Spring is the season of *planting* and the resurrection calls us to the true springtime of a fruitful and unselfish life.

O let us sow "beside all waters,"
Plant blessings and blessings will spring;
Sow truth and truth will grow.
Nor ever forget what a wonderful thing
Is the seed—the seed that we sow.

Seeking the Living among the Dead

Why do you look for the living among the dead? (Luke 24:5)

These women were looking for a dead Christ, and of course they could not find Him, for He was living. How often since have men sought for Christ where He could not be found! How sad is the long vigil of Israel's sons and daughters for the Messiah that does not come and never will come as they are looking for Him! Someday they will behold Him as the Living One and weep and wonder because so long they vainly sought Him in a false ideal among the dead hopes of their earthly national ambitions. So also Romish superstition paints the Christ with all the hideous and ghastly accompaniments of the crown of thorns, the pallid brow of death and the cerements of the tomb. There is no such Christ; "He is not here; he has risen!" (24:6). The crucifix is not the true symbol of redemption. That is the cross with the suffering Christ upon it; that is past and gone forever. Rather, the cross shining in the halo of the glory beyond and the crown above is the true symbol of Christianity.

Thorwaldsen, the great Norwegian sculptor, has cut in marble a group known as "The Cross and the Vine," in which the outlines of the cross are covered and almost lost in the luxuriant foliage and hanging clusters of a splendid vine that grows from the foot of the cross. The vine represents the living Christ and the fruits of His resurrection and life, obliterating almost the figure of the cross from whose roots all these blessings spring.

To many a Christian, Jesus is still but a dead Christ or at least an historic Christ, but not a living and present reality. The meaning of Easter is that Jesus is alive and is the Living Head of Christianity and the personal and intimate Friend of every true disciple, to whom He becomes revealed as his indwelling life and the source of all his strength and victory.

Do you know Him as the Living One? If you do not, Easter comes to you in vain with the sad cry of Mary: " 'They have taken my Lord away,' she said, 'and I don't know where they have put him' " (John 20:13).

You will observe in the story of the walk to

Emmaus that Jesus Christ was not recognized by the two disciples until they received Him into their house and sat down to eat and drink with Him. It was then that He was manifested to them and "they recognized him, and he disappeared from their sight" (Luke 24:31). While He merely walked with them by the way, they did not know Him; but when they took Him into the intimacy of their heart and home, then He was revealed to them as the Living One who had died upon the cross and had risen from the dead. And so, as you open the door of your heart and take Him as your guest and as your life, you too will know Him. The supreme epoch of every Christian life will have come in your experience, the great transition from the earthly to the heavenly, from the human to the divine, from the struggles and failures of man's finite strength to the infinite possibilities of God's best.

A Dead Christianity

The question of our text may be addressed to those who are following a dead Christianity, for a dead Christ brings a dead Christianity. Coleridge's dream of the Ancient Mariner, in which a phantom ship floats upon the silent ocean with a dead man at the helm, a dead man on the bridge and dead men standing at their posts as if frozen by one fatal breath into ice or marble, is only too real a picture of many a church with a dead man in the pulpit and dead men in the pews and the entire ritual that of a solemn funeral. The tasks and fasts and penances and ceremonial rites which constitute the religion of many people are but the cerements of the dead, the grave clothes which the Master threw away that morning when He rose. This is not Christianity. The true religion of Jesus robes itself in garments of love and liberty and joy, and goes forth to live for others and to bless the world.

It is remarkable that no mention is made of the Lord's apparel after His resurrection. We read of His seamless robe left behind Him when they nailed Him to the cross, and of the linen which they wrapped about Him at His burial and which they found, after His resurrection, neatly folded and laid away in the tomb. But nothing is said about His raiment as He appeared again and again to them. Is it not probably true that the robes He wore were part of His very flesh, a living drapery that grew as naturally as the flowers of Spring and the tints of the rainbow out of the glorified life that was springing within Him? These will be no doubt the garments our resurrection bodies will take on as part of our very organism, the beauty and glory of our inner life, and, like the sunlit clouds of heaven, will change every moment with new attractions and splendors. So true Christianity does not need to be dressed in the cowl of the monk and the vestments of the choir and the elaborate ceremonial of Ritualism and Romanism. Its appropriate dress is the garment of praise, the mantle of love and the girdle of service as it goes forth in the glory of resurrection life and heavenly love to represent the Master in this world of sin and sorrow, and stands like the ancient vision of Solomon, bright "like the dawn, fair as the moon, bright as the sun, majestic as the stars in procession" (Song of Songs 6:10). God give us this true Christian adorning and heavenly vestments, compared with which our Easter fashions are but as "filthy rags."

Dead Souls

The question of our text might be asked of those who are seeking for spiritual life among the dry bones of our fallen human nature. Oh, you who are trying to improve yourselves, to reform your lives, to build up your characters and to cultivate the fruits and grace of higher ethics and calling this religion, "Why do you look for the living among the dead?" (Luke 24:5).

Human nature is dead and beyond the power of self-improvement. God has simply provided for its burial and its resurrection life through the risen Christ. That is the meaning of this Easter day. The sentence of death has passed upon all man's best endeavors, and the only hope of our fallen race is the new birth and the resurrection life through Jesus Christ.

It is interesting to trace through the Scriptures the manifest truth that the first generation has always been a failure, and that it is the second birth that triumphs and remains. The first Adam fell; the second Adam achieved the destiny of humanity. The first Eden was lost forever, but the new heavens and the new earth shall bring back paradise restored. Eve's first son cruelly disappointed her; the second born and the third became the seed of promise. The old world passed out in the flood and the new world emerged under the arch of the rainbow on Mt. Ararat as a type of the great resurrection which Christ was to bring. Abraham's first born, Ishmael, had to be cast out, and in Isaac, his second born, his seed was called. Esau, the elder, gave place to Jacob, the younger; David, the youngest son of Jesse, was exalted above all his brethren as the Lord's anointed. In their journey to the Land of Promise, Israel's first generation failed; the second generation, consisting of their children, was chosen to enter in while the bones of their fathers were buried in the sands of the desert.

Even nature itself teaches us that a transformation must take place before the crawling worm can emerge from the chrysalis and become a soaring butterfly; the seed has to die and rot in the ground, and from its bosom comes forth the new germ that will bud and blossom and fill the earth with fruit. The tree that has but a natural birth must be grafted and cut down and wedded to a new branch before it can bear the best fruit. All nature is a parable of this mystery of mysteries.

If we look at the lives of some of the typical characters of the Bible, we shall see the same principle running through them. Jacob had to pass through the narrow gates of his great conflict at Peniel in order to come forth a new man with a new name, Israel, a prince with God. Job had to find out that all his natural goodness was insufficient and, in the keen light of God's revealing, cry, "I despise myself and repent in dust and ashes" (Job 42:6), before there came to him a new life and righteousness and blessing. Isaiah had to see himself as all unclean and then receive the cleansing coal of fire which sent him forth empowered for his great prophetic ministry. Simon Peter had to fall so far that he broke his own proud neck in the fall and then came forth from the wreck and the shame with a new and divine strength which enabled him to die at last with downward head on his Master's cross. Paul had to find out that all his righteousness was as dross and had to be clothed in the righteousness of Christ alone and make this his watchword: "I have been crucified with Christ and I no longer live, but Christ lives in me" (Galatians 2:20). This is the meaning of Easter. Have you entered into it and come forth with that death-born life?

A Dead Humanity

The question of our text might be asked of the people that are teaching in our day the sufficiency of earthly culture, education, fine art and humanitarianism to lift the race to its true plane and educate it out of its depravity and degeneracy. The world needs no sadder commentary on this stupendous folly than the late messages of poor Herbert Spencer to the world before he died, telling men of the best light that had come to him from the researches of eighty years, and then adding that the outlook for him, as he faced the great crisis of life, was dark and depressing indeed.

The world has tried it many times. Culture can never do more for humanity than it did for ancient Egypt, Greece and Babylonia or for modern Italy in the brightest hour of art. But alas, these were the darkest hours in the records of human crime! "Why do you look for the living among the dead?" (Luke 24:5). Humanity is like the dry bones of Ezekiel's vision, a moral cemetery, and nothing can lift it but the omnipotent touch of a divine resurrection.

A Lifeless World

The question of our text might be addressed to the people that are looking for happiness in this doomed world and trying to find their true life among the dead ashes of earthly pleasure. God says of such a person, "He feeds on ashes" (Isaiah 44:20). Ashes are just the wreckage of organic matter that has been consumed and the substance burned out of it. The world has nothing to give you but ashes. The world's heart has gone out since God has gone out, and righteousness is lost. Will love make earth a heaven? Read the records of modern divorce. Will fame last forever? Look at the overturning of all the tables of human ambition. Is wealth an antidote for every human ill? Look at the story of the colossal fortunes of our day and the disappointment, the oppression, the countless calamities that follow in their train. The story has not only been told, but lived ten thousand times, and to the end of the chapter the conclusion will still be the same. Expressed in the language of human philosophy and experience, it is found in the last words of one of earth's most successful men, "I have been everything and everything is nothing." Expressed in the language of the Bible and the testimony of the prince of earthly pleasure, power and even wisdom, it is "Vanity of vanities, all is vanity and vexation of spirit."

Oh, turn from the ash heaps of this desert of spiritual desolation and in yonder garden by the open grave learn the secret of a joy that will never fade. "Whoever drinks the water I give him will never thirst. Indeed, the water that I give him will become in him a spring of water welling up to eternal life" (John 4:14).

Dead Hopes

The question of our text speaks to the souls that are sitting in despair amid the dead hopes of their failures and disappointments. Rise up, despairing ones, bury your past in yonder grave; begin anew with Easter's dawning and know that the resurrection means for every discouraged man that God has established a great bankruptcy court where all the debts and losses of the past can be consigned to eternal oblivion and you can start anew with a heart as fresh and a hope as bright as if your life had this moment dropped from heaven, and you were not and never would be again the same man as he who wrought the sin, the shame, the failure and the wreck that lies behind you. Leave it at the cross and rise up and take the fortune that He has purchased for you and is waiting to give you as the gift of His free and sovereign grace.

Someone tells of an old man who was riding through a country district when he was accosted by a native who asked him for a ride. He soon began to talk to the man and found that he was not saved. The native asked him after a while what his business was in those parts.

He replied, "I represent a very large estate that has just been divided by the will of the testator and some of the heirs live around here, and I am looking for them. Their family name begins with the letter 'S,' and they are a very large family." Immediately the man became greatly interested.

"Why," he said, "I know some of them; they are the Smiths, are they not?"

"No," said the man, as he looked him earnestly in the face. "Their name is 'Sinner,' and I think you are one of them, and I have come to bring you a fortune."

That is the meaning of this bright Easter morning. The Friend who loved you before you were born, has paid all your debts, has discharged your liabilities, has blotted out your past, and He brings you an inheritance of love and hope and everlasting joy which you may freely have by accepting His grace and giving yourself to Him in loving return.

Our Holy Dead

Finally, the angels bear this message to some who are living among the tombs of their earthly bereavements and thinking of their loved ones as dead. They are not here; "Why do you look for the living among the dead?" (Luke 24:5).

The pathetic story is told of two little children who, after the death of their mother, were digging a hole in the garden with their feeble hands. When asked why, they explained that they were digging a way to heaven to find mother. Someone had told them, when they saw her body lowered into the dark, cold ground, that she had gone to heaven, and they thought that heaven was somewhere in the ground.

Alas, how many hearts are buried there. This is the very opposite of what God has intended. He has taken your loved ones in order to lift your hearts to that heavenly home where they are risen and rejoicing now, and to help us to realize that world which is the true goal of all our hopes and the only changeless home where parted friends shall meet again. "Why do you look for the living among the dead?" (24:5). Arise and live with Him in the things above.

And so we might apply at greater length this searching question to all the things that we are vainly searching for below the skies. Lift up your eyes, lift up your hearts, look forward and

remember that "the time comes for God to restore everything" (Acts 3:21). This is to come not
here but by and by when Jesus comes. Even much
that we have prayed for, believed for and
spiritually attained only in part is waiting for us
yonder. Then shall come back to us all we have
sacrificed and surrendered here. And this
universe itself shall complete the mystery of the
resurrection by passing through the ordeal of the
last conflagration and shall come forth with the
same mark of resurrection upon it that God is
putting upon each of us now. Then, indeed it
shall be true that He that sits upon the throne
shall say, "I am making everything new!" (Revelation 21:5).

Dear friend, are you living in this new world
and for this coming age? There are two races
crossing the narrow path of time. One is the
Adam race, the other is the Christ race; one is the
earthly race, the other is the heavenly race; one is
doomed to remain among the dead, the other is
pressing on to immortality and glory. "As was the
earthly man, so are those who are of the earth;
and as is the man from heaven, so also are those
who are of heaven. And just as we have borne the
likeness of the earthly man, so shall we bear the
likeness of the man from heaven" (1 Corinthians
15:48–49). Beloved, come from among the dead
and live forevermore.

The Power of the Resurrection

*After his suffering, he showed himself to
these men and gave many convincing proofs
that he was alive. He appeared to them over
a period of forty days and spoke about the
kingdom of God. (Acts 1:3)*

Our Lord's earthly life may be divided into
three sections: before His passion, during
His passion and the forty-day interval between
His resurrection and ascension.

Like the afterglow in an Oriental sky still shining long after the sun has disappeared, or like the
Indian summer with its soft light and lingering
sunshine, these days seem to have about them a
mystic glory halfway between the earthly and the
heavenly. His feet still touched the earth, but His
head was in the heavens.

The story of those days is but partly told, but we know enough to afford us seven distinct messages from the departing Master.

The Reality and Significance of the Resurrection

It is strange that this should need to be demonstrated to Christian disciples, but it is the church of Christ that today is beginning to discredit the physical reality of the Lord's resurrection. Therefore, God had made it a demonstrable fact supported by "many convincing proofs" (Acts 1:3): the Roman guards who were stationed around the tomb, and whose silly lie about the stealing of His body, was the very best proof that that body had gone; the angel messengers who repeatedly announced that He was risen indeed; His repeated appearings to His disciples and the testimony of Thomas in spite of his own skepticism. These form but a little part of the chain of evidence that so acute a mind as Paul's considered unanswerable and that the profoundest judicial minds today have declared to be absolutely conclusive.

The nature of Christ's resurrection is as clear as the fact is certain. The picture given by the evangelist leaves no doubt of the absolute identity of the Christ of Easter with the Crucified of Calvary and the Man of Galilee. The very marks of the nails and the spear were visible and tangible. So real was His humanity that they could handle Him and know by the evidence of their senses that he had actual flesh and bones, and that He could eat the broiled fish they set before Him and distinguish the taste of the honeycomb as well. But so transcendently more mighty was His resurrection state than even His former physical life that His body could pass through the closed door and the stone that sealed the sepulcher without hindrance, and could rise and ascend to heaven in defiance of the law of gravitation without the faintest effort.

The significance of His resurrection is impossible to exaggerate. It is the fundamental proof of His Messiahship and of the truth of Christianity. It is the evidence of our justification. It is the source of our sanctification. It is the guarantee of our future resurrection. It is the pledge of all power that we can ever need in this present life. And it is the pattern according to which faith may claim the "mystery of his will according to his good pleasure, which he purposed in Christ" (Ephesians 1:9).

The Abiding Presence of Our Risen Lord

This is assured by His own announcement, every word of which is weighted with such force and suggestiveness, "Lo, I am with you alway," or literally, "all the days, even unto the end of the world [age]" (Matthew 28:20, KJV). The importance of the announcement is attested by the first word, "Lo," which calls attention to its extraordinary significance. The identity of His presence with His life on earth is emphasized by the present tense of the verb, "I am with you." It was not a promise of some future visitation, but a presence that never should be withdrawn. And the beautiful translation, "all the days," makes that presence as perpetual and as new as the dawn of each succeeding day. He is present throughout all the vicissitudes of life's changes and trials. The promise is not "all the years," but "all the days"— every day and every sort of day: the cloudy days as well as the sunny ones; the days of trouble as well as the days of blessing; the lonely days, the days of weakness and even failure—"all the days, even unto the end of the age."

And as if this announcement was not sufficient, He illustrated it by several manifestations which seem to be prophetic of the way He might still be expected to show Himself to His earthly followers. How unspeakably precious is the picture of His walk to Emmaus with the two disciples. How touching is the delicacy with which He acted as though He would have gone farther, and waited to be pressed to tarry in their home. How gladly He accepted the pressing invitation. How gloriously He manifested Himself in the breaking of the bread, and then how tactfully He vanished when the vision would have disturbed them from their simple life of faith if it had been further prolonged. So still He meets us along life's pathway. So still He sometimes unveils His glorious face. So still He quickly lets fall the curtain and leaves us to walk by faith and not by sight. How full of pathos is His message immediately after His resurrection:

"But go, tell [my] disciples and Peter" (Mark 16:7). So still He singles out the timid, the discouraged and the fallen. How full of comfort is that early morning visitation on the shore of the Galilean sea when the disciples had toiled all night and caught nothing; and the gray dawn found the Master there to supply their physical necessity and help them in their temporal distress, and then to lead them on to the higher lessons of suffering and service. It is in the light of these object lessons that we are ever to interpret that shining and everlasting promise, "Lo, I am with you [all the days]" (Matthew 28:20).

The Importance of His Word as the Vehicle of His Presence

It was as He talked with the disciples by the way and opened the Scriptures that their hearts first began to burn within them. He impressed upon them the prophetic word of which His sufferings and glory were the one continual burden. It is in His Word that we shall always find the Master near us. The warning of the beloved John concerning them that seduce us is that we are to continue in the Word which we have heard from the beginning. Spiritual manifestations are not always divine visitations. The test of every experience and of every spirit is the Word of Jesus Christ.

The Promise and the Presence of the Holy Spirit

How often this promise was repeated during

the forty days. How imperatively they were bidden to tarry for His power. And yet the Lord
began even before His ascension to anticipate the
coming Pentecost. As He breathed upon them,
He commanded them to "receive the Holy
Spirit" (John 20:22). So still the Holy Spirit is a
present fact, and no believer need wait a single
day for His coming, but the fullness of the Spirit
is a larger promise and experience. As we wait for
His infilling, there are heights and depths of
power and blessing which are but as the pebbles
on the shore compared with the mighty deep
which lies beyond.

These after-Easter days should be for each of
us days of the Holy Spirit, days of waiting for a
deeper filling, a mightier baptism, a larger room
for His incoming and a larger work for His outgoing through our lips and hands and feet and
lives. Shall we take this blessed promise in its forcible, literal phrasing and prove it in both of its
meanings, "I am going to send you what my
Father has promised; but stay in the city until you
have been clothed with power from on high"
(Luke 24:49)? The sending has already begun.
The receiving is already in process. The ending is
on its way. But the largeness of the blessing
demands more than a passing moment, more
than a formal prayer, more than a hurried meal at
a quick lunch counter; it demands even days of
waiting on the Lord, nights of intense communion, and all the days and all the years of our
earthly lives to give sufficient room and time for

us to take in the whole significance of that mighty promise "that you may be filled to the measure of all the fullness of God" (Ephesians 3:19).

The Call to Service: The Great Commission

The Master's parting messages justified no dream of selfish spiritual enjoyment, but called for the most strenuous service for the souls of men and the kingdom of God. Here are some flashes of light upon the life of service as the Lord has outlined it: "Feed my lambs" (John 21:15); "Take care of my sheep" (21:16); "Shepherd my feeble sheep." And again, "As the Father has sent me, I am sending you" (20:21). We are sent ones, we are apostles, we are ambassadors. We are not here because of our earthly citizenship, but because we have come, like our Lord, from heaven where our spirits were born to witness for Him on earth. And preeminent above all other ministries is the Great Commission for the evangelization of the heathen world. The command, "Go into all the world and preach the good news to all creation" (Mark 16:15) requires a personal ministry from man to man and for every man beneath the sky. The command to begin "in Jerusalem" (Acts 1:8) passes on to us the great trust for the chosen people. "Go . . . and make disciples of all nations" (Matthew 28:19) raises the commission to a nobler plane and makes us ambassadors from the King of kings and trustees of the gospel for every kindred and tribe and tongue. The command, "You will be my witnesses in Jerusalem, and in all Judea and Samaria, and to the ends of the earth" (Acts 1:8) lifts the outlook beyond any section of humanity, any circle of selfish patriotism, any form of religious selfishness, and makes the work of evangelization the one supreme ministry of the church of Christ and the one paramount responsibility of every disciple of the Lord Jesus Christ. You certainly have not come into close touch with the risen Christ or caught the spirit of those last momentous days on earth if you are still inactive, indifferent or even neutral in this mighty enterprise which is the emergency work of our times and which is the one great business for which God has called and blessed us.

The Meaning of the Ascension

At length the forty days were ended, and in the simple story we are told that He led them out as far as Bethany and lifted up His hands and blessed them. "While he was blessing them, he left them and was taken up into heaven" (Luke 24:51). It is sweet to remember that the last attitude of the Lord Jesus on earth was that of stretching out His pierced hands in loving benediction. As He rose higher and higher in silent majesty, their last remembrance of Him would be that shining face and those outstretched and gracious hands.

It was necessary that He should pass from the earthly scene and return to His native heaven. The disciples must know, the world must know, the ages to come must know that this little planet is

not all of God's great universe. Away beyond the
blue dome of heaven, beyond the circling horizon,
beyond the rising and the setting sun, beyond the
stars of light, beyond the last gasp of dying agony,
the moldering grave and the mourner's tear—
there is another realm, there is a greater and a better world, there is a home above, there is a heavenly land, the home of God and the great metropolis
of His mighty universe. And when He had passed
through every stage of earthly experience from the
cradle to the grave, He passed on and took His
place at the right hand of God amid glorious angels and ransomed men. It was necessary that the
children of God should realize through the ascension of their living Head that this old earth is not
their home; but, like their Master's, their citizenship, too, is in heaven. The ascension of Jesus
Christ shifts our center of gravity, our meridian of
latitude and longitude, our pole star of hope and
expectation from earth to heaven.

But Christ's ascension meant much more for
Him and us. It meant a new and higher ministry
for Him. It meant His heavenly priesthood as our
Representative and Intercessor before the throne,
presenting our worthless names with acceptance
to His Father, presenting our imperfect prayers
with the incense of His merits, and saving us by
His life as He had already saved as by His death.
It meant His glorious kingship as Head over all
things for His body, the church. There He sits
enthroned above all principality and power and
every name that is named, ruling and overruling,

conquering and to conquer, King of kings and
Lord of lords, completing His church and
preparing for His coming. Christ's ascension and
ministry on high was just as necessary as His life
on earth, His death on Calvary and His resurrection on Easter morning.

> Where high the heavenly temple stands,
> A house of God not made with hands,
> A great High priest our nature wears,
> The Guardian of mankind appears.
>
> He who for men their surety stood,
> And poured on earth His precious
>   blood,
> Pauses in heaven the mighty plan,
> The Saviour and the Friend of man.

The Hope of His Coming

The Master Himself had passed from view and
the last echoes of His voice in benediction had
died away, when suddenly another voice fell upon
their ears, the voice of two celestial angels. Up
yonder a chariot cloud had received the ascend-
ing Lord, perhaps a cloud of innumerable angels,
so high above the earth that their forms could not
be distinguished and they appeared to mortal
vision like a distant veil of mist. But for a moment
the Savior lingered behind that cloud and sent
from the heavenly retinue that had come to at-
tend Him home two special messengers to bear

His postscript to His loved disciples. And it was this. "This same Jesus, who has been taken from you into heaven, will come back in the same way you have seen him go into heaven" (Acts 1:11).

Having sailed once from New York harbor for an absence of many months, I well remember that just as the boat was about to leave the harbor, a messenger came to take ashore the last greetings of the passengers. There was only time for just a word, but that word from most of us was "Back soon." And that sweet hope cheered through the long months of parting the waiting hearts at home. This was the Master's thought as He left the harbor of time, on that old spring noontime on the hillside of Bethany: I have left you for a little while, but I will see you again and your hearts shall rejoice.

That is the goal, that is the outlook, that is the perspective of faith and hope—not the cross, not even the resurrection, not the work of missions, not even the blessed presence of the Master and the power of the Holy Spirit. All these only lead up to that transcendent and eternal hope,

> That one faroff divine event
> To which the whole creation moves.

Is that the goal to which you are moving? Have you inscribed on every friendship, every investment, every undertaking, every work, every joy and every sorrow, "Till the coming of the Lord" (1 Thessalonians 4:15)?

10

After-Easter Days

*After his suffering, he showed himself to
these men and gave many convincing proofs
that he was alive. He appeared to them over
a period of forty days, and spoke about the
kingdom of God. (Acts 1:3)*

Easter morning is the beginning of a unique
and most tenderly interesting portion of
our blessed Savior's life. It is the transition period
between His earthly ministry and His heavenly
exaltation. Like the Indian summer of the year,
there is a tender veil of loveliness and mystery
about it which links it with both worlds, and
makes it a peculiarly appropriate pattern of a life
hid with Christ in God, in which we may walk
with Him all our days with our heads in heaven,
while our feet still tread the earth below. May the
Holy Spirit vividly reveal to us such glimpses of

this blessed life as will enable us to reproduce it in our own experience and to walk with Him with a new sense of His abiding presence and glorious reality!

A Living Christ

This glad resurrection morning dispels from the religion of Jesus all the shadow of the sepulcher and all the morbid atmosphere of sorrow, depression and death. The Christ of true Christianity is not a bleeding, thorn-crowned *Ecce Homo*, but a gold and radiant face, bright as the springtime morning and radiant with immortal life. "I am the Living One; I was dead," is His message, and "Behold I am alive for ever and ever!" (Revelation 1:18). Oh, may this day impress upon our hearts the reality of a risen and living Christ, until He shall be more actual to us than any other personality; and we shall know what it means to be not only "reconciled to him through the death of his Son," but "shall we be saved through his life!" (Romans 5:10).

A Victorious Christ

What a picture of easy and uttermost triumph is that resurrection scene! Satan had done his utmost; men had done their best to hold the Captive of the tomb. But without an effort the mighty Sleeper calmly rose before the Easter dawn, deliberately laying off the grave clothes and wrapping up the napkin, and putting all in place as naturally as any of us this morning arranged our bedroom. Then through that colossal stone that closed His tomb, He passed without even rolling it aside or breaking the seal. And before the guards could know that He was risen, He was standing calmly in the garden, talking with Mary as though nothing had happened. The infinite facility with which He put His feet on every foe and rose above every obstacle is, perhaps, the most overwhelming impression we have received from all the incidents of His resurrection.

So, too, we see the same victorious power expressed in the attitude of the angel who followed Him, and with a single touch rolled away the stone from the sepulcher and coolly sat down upon it, and then looked in the faces of the keepers till they grew pale with terror and flew in horror and dismay without a struggle.

Such is our risen Christ still, the mighty Victor over all His foes and ours. Could we see Him now, we would behold Him sitting on His Father's throne, undismayed by all the powers of darkness, and "since that time he waits for his enemies to be made his footstool" (Hebrews 10:13). Oh, how it cheers our timid hearts to behold our glorious and victorious Captain, and to hear Him say of every adversary and every difficulty, "I have overcome for you." God help us to see the Captain as Joshua beheld Him, and before Him the walls of every Jericho will fall and the legions of every opposing force will melt away!

A Simple Christ

How natural, how easy, how artless His manifestations were through those blessed forty days! How quietly He dropped down among them, unheralded, unassuming, unattended by angelic guards, and sometimes undistinguished from themselves in His simple presence! Look at Him as He meets with Mary in that first morning interview, standing like an ordinary stranger in the garden, speaking to her in easy conversation. " 'Woman,' he said, 'why are you crying? Who is it you are looking for?' " (John 20:15). And then, when the moment for recognition comes, He speaks to her heart in the one artless word of personal and unutterable love which disarmed all her amazement and fear, and brought back all the old recollections and affections of her throbbing heart! See Him again on the way to Emmaus! How naturally He drops in upon the little company as they walk! How unaffectedly He talks with them! How easily He turns the conversation to heavenly themes, and yet how free from strain His every attitude and word! All they are conscious of is a strange burning in their hearts and a kindling warmth of love. At length they constrain Him and He allows Himself to be pressed to enter in. He sits down by their table, He eats bread, as if He had been another disciple like themselves; and only then, as He vanishes quietly from their sight, do they realize that it is the Lord.

And yet again, on the shores of Tiberias, how exquisite is His approach! How natural His greeting; how easy the mighty miracle of the draught of fishes; how calm and unaffected is the meeting as they reach the shore and the simple breakfast in which He Himself takes part! How exquisite the interview with Simon Peter, the delicacy and tenderness of which no word can ever express! Oh, what a picture of that Blessed One who still lives to be our constant Visitor, our ceaseless Companion and Friend, who meets us like Mary in our hours of sorrow, who walks with us, as with them, often unrecognized at first, who greets us in the cold, sad morning after our long hours of waiting and toil and failure with His marvelous deliverance and yet more gracious words of love and instruction. So near is He that not even our nearest friends can come so close! So simple is He that His messages come as the intuition of our own hearts; and yet He is the wonderful Counselor and the mighty God for all our perplexities and all our hard places. *Blessed Christ of the forty days, oh, help us, with a faith more simple and a love more childlike to walk with You!*

The Mighty Christ

It is hard for us to realize the presence that comes with such gentle footsteps and undemonstrative simplicity; but back of that gentle form and those noiseless steps is the omnipotence that could say, "All authority [power, KJV] in heaven and on earth has been given to me" (Matthew 28:18). *All power is His in heaven.* He is the lamb in the midst of the Throne, that holds in His hand the seven seals and unrolls the scroll of destiny and providence for all worlds and beings and events. All the mighty acts of God recorded in the Old Testament were but manifestations of His power. All the mighty movements which began with His ascension are the workings of His hands. All the movements of Divine providence are subject to His command. All the mighty angels of heaven's myriad hosts are subject to His bidding. All the powers of hell tremble at His name! All the promises of God are fulfilled with His endorsement. All the laws of nature are subject to His mandates.

And *all power on earth is subordinate to His power.* Not a wind can blow without His permission, not a disease can strike but as He allows, not a human hand can hurt us while He shields us with His presence. The circumstances of life, the enemies of our souls and the infirmities of our bodies are subject to His Word. The very thrones of earth are subordinate to His authority. He can make a Cyrus send back the tribes of Israel by a national decree. He can make a Constantine behold the flaming Cross upon the sky and become a follower of the Heavenly Standard. He can open nations and kingdoms to the gospel, and so He bids us go forth and disciple all the nations because of His almighty power in our behalf!

How mighty was the power of the resurrection! It surmounted the power of death and the grave;

it passed through the solid stone; it defied the stamp of the Roman government and the sentinels of the Roman army. It could pass through the closed doors without rending them asunder. It could bring the miraculous draught of fishes to the apostle's net with a single word of command. It could rise without an effort in the chariot of His ascension. It could anoint those weak and timid men with the power that shook the world and laid the foundations of the church.

Oh, that our eyes were but opened that we might behold

> . . . the riches of his glorious inheritance in the saints and his incomparably great power for us who believe. That power is like the working of his mighty strength, which he exerted in Christ when he raised him from the dead and seated him at his right hand in the heavenly realms, far above all rule and authority, power and dominion, and every title that can be given, not only in the present age but also in the one to come. And God placed all things under his feet and appointed him to be head over everything for the church, which is his body, the fullness of him who fills everything in every way. (Ephesians 1:18–23)

Why is it that we do not receive and realize more of this Almighty Christ? Alas! because we cannot understand or stand the fullness of His power. God is ready to work through us the triumphs of His omnipotence, but we must be fitted vessels, open to His touch and able to stand His power. The ordinance that has to bear a mighty charge of powder must be heavy enough to stand the charge without explosion. And so hearts that are to know the power of Him "who is able to do immeasurably more than all we ask or imagine" (Ephesians 3:20) must be "[strengthened] . . . with power through his Spirit in [their] inner being so that Christ may dwell in [their] hearts through faith" (3:16–17). To think of what Christ is ready and willing to do in us and for us would frighten some of us into apoplexy, and actually to realize it would snap the frail thread of life itself. Christ's heart is bursting with resources that the world needs and that He is ready to use if only He could find vessels ready and willing to use them.

Oh, that we had the courage to see the power which He is waiting to place at the service of all who are consecrated enough to use it for His glory and close enough to receive the heavenly baptism! He has for us the power of the Holy Spirit, the power of prayer, the power that will conquer circumstances and control all events for His will, and the power that will make us the trophies of His grace and the monuments of His indwelling presence and victory.

We shall find this power as we go forth to use it according to His own commission, "Therefore go and make disciples of all nations" (Matthew

28:19). Nothing but a work as wide as the world can ever make room for the power which Christ is waiting to bestow.

A Loving Christ

How unavailing all His power would be if we were not sure that it is available for us, and that His heart as tenderly loves us as His mighty hand can help us! How tender and loving the Christ of the forty days! See Him in the garden as He speaks to Mary with tender sympathy: " 'Woman,' he said, 'why are you crying? Who is it you are looking for?' " (John 20:15), He asks, and then calls her by her name in tones which must have expressed more than words could tell. What mourner can doubt henceforth His sympathy and love? What heart can hesitate to accept His friendship which still speaks to each of us with as direct and personal a call, and gives to each a name of special and affectionate regard?

Or look again at Him as He meets with Thomas, the doubting one, the willful disciple that petulantly demanded that the Lord should meet him with an evidence that He had given to none other, and that no human heart had a right imperiously to claim. But how tenderly the Lord concedes even his demand, until Thomas is ashamed to accept it and, more amazed at his Lord's magnanimity and omniscience than the evidence of His wounds, he cries, "My Lord and my God!" (20:28). Who that is harassed with doubts and difficulties need fear again to bring

them to His presence? Who with such conde-
scending love is ready to meet them all, and to
make our hearts know by the deeper evidence of
His own great love and the revealing of Himself
that He is indeed the Son of God?

And look at His interview with Simon Peter!
What backslider need ever doubt again the
Savior's forgiving love, or fear to come and know
that he will be welcomed to a nearer place in His
heart and a higher service in His kingdom if only
he can say as Simon said, "Lord, you know all
things; you know that I love you" (21:17).

So tender, so forgiving, so full of love He comes
to us, to dry our tears, to satisfy our doubts, to forgive our failures, to restore our souls, and then to
use us for a higher service, just because we have
learned through our own infirmities the depths of
His great love. The secret of walking closely with
Christ and working successfully for Him is to fully
realize that we are His beloved. Let us but feel that
He has set His heart upon us, that He is watching
us from those heavens with the same tender interest that He felt for Simon and Mary, that He is
working out the mystery of our lives with the same
solicitude and fondness, that He is following us
day by day as any mother follows her babe in his
first attempt to walk alone, that He has set His
love upon us, and, in spite of ourselves, is working
out for us His highest will and blessing, as far as
we will let Him, and then nothing can discourage
us. Our hearts will glow with responsive love. Our
faith will spring to meet His mighty promises, and

our sacrifices shall become the very luxuries of love for one so dear. This was the secret of John's spirit. "We know and rely on the love God has for us" (1 John 4:16). And the heart that has fully learned this has found the secret of unbounded faith and enthusiastic service.

The Physical Christ

He that came forth from Joseph's tomb came forth in the flesh, with a material body and the same form that He had laid down in death and the grave. He made this most emphatic in His interview with His disciples after His resurrection. He wished them to be thoroughly assured that there was no illusion about His body. "Touch me and see," was His emphatic word, "a ghost does not have flesh and bones, as you see I have" (Luke 24:39).

Indeed, His spiritual consciousness had not died; it was only His body that tasted death, and it was His body therefore that was raised from death. The resurrection of Christ, then, is a physical fact, and the physical meaning of the resurrection must be of surpassing importance. It means no less than this, that He has come forth to be the physical life of His people now, and in a little while the Fountain of their immortality and the Head of their resurrection bodies.

What a source of strength and inspiration it is for us to know that our blessed Lord has still the same physical organization that we possess, and is willing and able to share with these mortal frames

His infinite and quickening life! He is our living Bread, and as He lived by the Father, so we may live by Him, and not only is He the source of health and strength to our material life, but He cares for the wants of the body. The disciples were hungry and cold from their fruitless fishing that Galilean morning; He saw their need and tenderly asked them, "Friends, haven't you any fish?" (John 21:5) and then, filling their empty nets and spreading the table on the shore, He said, "Come and have breakfast" (21:12). So still He thinks of the poor and the struggling, the hungry and the helpless ones, and stands beside them in their need, ready and able, by a word, to provide immediate and abundant supply.

Are we today in any place of need? The Christ of the forty days is nearer than we think, able to "sympathize with our weaknesses" (Hebrews 4:15), and ready to give us the greatest help in time of need. Like the fishermen of that Galilean sea, our empty nets can be filled at His bidding; the perplexed workman can be directed to the very thing to do; the wretched failure can be all corrected. There is no need that he cannot supply, no counsel that He is not able to give, no regions where His power does not penetrate, no disciple that He does not love to help in every time of need. Oh, let us trust Him more with all our circumstances and sorrows, and our utmost need will only prove the more infinite resources of His love and grace.

The Ever-Present Christ

The Christ of the forty days is not a transient vision that has passed away forever, but the Christ of all the ages. Standing at the close of those blessed days midway between earth and heaven, He said, "I am with you always, to the very end of the age" (Matthew 28:20). That blessed present tense has bridged the past and the present, and has prolonged those heavenly days after the resurrection through all the days since then. It is not "I will be," as one who has to go away and come back again, but "I am," as a presence that is never to be withdrawn. He is unseen, it is true, but is as real as any friend is real in his absence as well as presence. For in the spiritual world, distance and time are eliminated. Just as the telescope can bring the distant object near the eye, and the telephone can present the voice that is hundreds of miles away to the listening and attentive ear, so there is a spiritual mechanism that can make Christ as immediate to the heart as though He were still visibly by our side. Had we but another sense, all heavenly beings and realities would be directly present to our perception.

The promise of this beautiful passage is not only fulfilled in the presence of Christ in the heart of the believer, which is a literal and glorious truth, but it is a presence *with us*. It is more than the spiritual consciousness of the Lord's indwelling. It is His direct personality and constant companionship with all our life and His omnipotent cooperation in all our needs. It is the presence of One who has all power in heaven and in earth, and whose presence means the defeat of every adversary, the solution of every difficulty, the supply of every need.

Oh, it does seem, in these days, as though we could almost see Him moving in the midst of His people, here and there, in His mighty working, on the mission field with the one worker in the midst of dangers and foes, in the busy streets of the crowded city, in the mingled incidents of business life, in the whirl and confusion of our intense life today, in every department of human society—touching with His hands all the chords of influence and power, moving the wheels of providence, and working out His purpose for His people and the redemption of the world. Oh, that we might see Him as Joshua saw the Captain when He entered Canaan and camped around Jericho, as Stephen saw Him when he faced the crowd of wolfish foes that thirsted for his blood, as Paul saw Him amid the tempests of the Adriatic and the lions of the Coliseum, as John saw Him in the midst of the Throne, holding in His hand the seven stars and walking in the midst of the seven golden lampstands, and then standing before the Throne with all the seals of human destiny in His own right hand! Then, indeed, no trial could discourage us, no foe intimidate us, no fear dismay us, no work overwhelm us; for above every voice of peril or of hostile power, we would hear His gentle whisper, "I am with you always, to the very end of the age" (28:20).

The promise is better translated "all the days," rather than "always." He comes to you each day with a new blessing. Every morning, day by day, He walks with us, with a love that never tires and a blessing that never grows old. And He is with us "all the days"; it is a ceaseless abiding. There is no day so dark, so commonplace, so uninteresting, but you find Him there. Often, no doubt, He is unrecognized, as He was on the way to Emmaus, until you realize how your heart has been warmed, your love stirred and your Bible so strangely vivified that every promise seems to speak to you with heavenly reality and power. It was the Lord! God grant that His living presence may be made more and more real to us all henceforth; and whether we have the consciousness and evidence, as they had a few glorious times those forty days, or whether we go forth into the coming days, as they did most of their days, to walk by simple faith and in simple duty, let us know, at least, that the fact is true forevermore, that *He is with us*, a presence all unseen but real, and ready if we need Him any moment to manifest Himself for our relief.

There is a beautiful incident related of the mother of an English schoolboy whom, when he was a lad, she sent to a boarding school, some distance from her home, where the rules of the school only permitted her to visit once a fortnight. But this was more than her mother heart could stand, and so, all unknown to her boy or his teachers, she rented a little attic overlooking the school, and often, when he little dreamed, she would sit in that upper room with her eyes on her darling boy as he played in that yard below or studied in the schoolroom. He could not see her, nor did he dream that she was there, but had he cried or called her name or needed her for a moment, he was within her reach.

This is little parable of the sleepless love and the ceaseless oversight which our Savior exercises toward His beloved ones, for He has His eye upon us by day and by night. And although we do not see His face and hands and form as He moves through our pathway, dissipating our foes and clearing our way, yet He is there—ever there "all the days, even unto the end." Let us believe His promise; let us assume the reality of His presence; let us recognize Him as ever near; let us speak to Him as one ever by our side; and He shall ever answer us, either by the whispers of His love or by the workings of His hand.

Thus shall we never be alone; thus shall we never be defenseless; thus shall we never be defeated; thus need we never fear. And even should the lonely vale itself open to us, it shall be but the opening vista of a larger vision and a close and nearer presence, as we find "that neither death nor life, neither angels nor demons, neither the present nor the future, nor any powers, neither height nor depth, nor anything else in all creation, will be able to separate us from the love of God that is in Christ Jesus our Lord" (Romans 8:38–39).

SCRIPTURE INDEX

In his lifetime, A.B. Simpson wrote and published over 100 books. Christian Publications is committed to bringing back into print all of his books that have relevance to a contemporary audience—approximately 80 books. The following titles are currently available through your local Christian bookstore:

The Best of A.B. Simpson
The Christ in the Bible Commentary
Volume 1 (Genesis-Deuteronomy)
Volume 2 (Joshua-Chronicles)
Volume 3 (The Kings and Prophets, Psalms, Isaiah)
Volume 4 (Matthew-Acts)
Volume 5 (Romans-Colossians)
Volume 6 (Thessalonians-Revelation, Index)
Christ in the Tabernacle
The Christ Life
Danger Lines in the Deeper Life
Days of Heaven on Earth
The Fourfold Gospel
The Gentle Love of the Holy Spirit
The Gospel of Healing
The Holy Spirit (Volumes 1 and 2)
A Larger Christian Life
The Life of Prayer
Missionary Messages
The Names of Jesus
The Self-Life and the Christ-Life
When the Comforter Came
Wholly Sanctified